Praise for David and Myra Vandy's
SMOOTH TRANSITIONS 4 TEENS
And their lifetime of work on behalf of Youth

Strengthen Community, Securing the Future for our Youth

"I know of no people who have gone as far in committing their lives to the well-being of kids and families than David and Myra Vandy. Not only have they taken them into their home. They have gone into big dormitories full of them! The Vandys have devoted much energy and many hours, days, months, and years developing meaningful materials to guide them in their lives. They have strengthened neighborhoods and schools to become more sensitive and supportive to their kids. Indeed, David and Myra have increased the capacity of states to serve children and youth more effectively."
J. U. Foster Care Agency Owner, WI

"I found both David and Myra to be highly motivated, creative thinkers and planners. It was very evident that they possess the talents and skills to design and implement a wide variety of programming for staff and youth. They were able to improve and expand our relationship with many providers and local residents. They initiated grant donations and community projects, which will have a long-term benefit to our organization. Both David and Myra possess the rare combination of administrative and programming skills." D.P. Youth Agency Administrator, NC

"I have known Mr. and Mrs. Vandy for 20 years. I have found them to be individuals of integrity, honesty, and compassion with a deep-felt commitment and passion for giving back. These characteristics guide their lives and the work they have devoted their lives to. Everywhere they share of themselves, they leave a positive and enduring impact."
D.L. Youth Agency Administrator, NM

"I want to thank you for all you have done for me. I know God put you in my life for a reason, and it is because I really never had that type of encouragement, that helped. I'm so blessed and honored to meet the most amazing people. I will never forget you because you two made me believe that there is a purpose in my life." B.S., Youth, NC

"The Northside Planning Council is pleased to honor David and Myra Vandy in recognition of their outstanding leadership and dedicated service to their Neighborhood Association and their role in helping Madison's Northside win recognition as national "Neighborhood of the Year" for our collective efforts to improve the quality of life for all residents of our Northside neighborhoods." - Northside Planning Council- WI

"David and Myra have a gift. They have an amazing ability to realize a vision and will not accept anything less than the best possible result." B.W., Counselor, NC

"Thanks guys! Thanks for all your efforts in creating this SMOOTH TRANSITIONS 4 TEENS tool, which can help students realize some of their goals. You would be pleased to know C.S. will be using SMOOTH TRANSITIONS 4 TEENS in our new community-based classroom at Cottonwood Mall. He has a desire and know-how to implement the integrity of your effort. Best wishes to both of you again." S.F., Educator, NM

"Our boys look forward to graduating high school with the information they need to be self-sufficient. Dave and Myra Vandy are a wealth of hope for that journey." S.G., Foster Parent, WI

"Well, it's been 7 months since you came and changed our little world. We have seen an increase in consistency with staff, which in turn brings compliance and a pleasant home atmosphere to our group home shelter. Staff have something solid and reliable to implement as a team and all move in the same direction. Thank you again for all your help and training. It was nice to be trained by someone who could relate to the realities of group living." P.W., Crisis Shelter Administrator, NM

"Whew, where do I even start this? What do I even say? First off, if you ever get the chance to meet this wonderfully caring and passionate couple then you can understand why this is hard for me. I want everyone to know that if they say they care about you, then they really do. Their words aren't just words, they are words that turn to actions. How do I know? Well, they were a huge part of my life in the sense of finding myself as a person. They helped me realize that being whoever I wanted to be in life is ok, and to follow and believe what I wanted. Never would they ever question what I liked or say anything negative about it either. They truly are what you call a power couple, and if there was ever a problem you couldn't deal with on your own, they were there to help you in any way possible. I love these two like you wouldn't believe. So, if anyone knows people, well, they do. They know what helps a person love themselves when you feel like no one else does, or when you feel like everything is crashing down right in front of you. I love the Vandys, and I couldn't be any happier knowing I've met these two while being alive, and I thank them for showing me that "Its ok to be yourself ". Love you two♡♡" M.T., Youth, NC

"You helped me grow as a person and the things you taught me helped to make my life a little easier. You were a guide to me when I could trust no one else, helping me deal with a lot of personal issues and understanding me when no one else could. I was never one to open up to people, but for some reason, I could always open up to you. You could relate to how I felt and understood the perspective I was coming from. You helped me grow and mend relationships that were broken years ago. I can't write enough on how you have helped me, and you know the respect I feel for you. Thank you for everything along the path of my life."

M.L., WI High School Teacher, Champion High School Basketball Coach, Courageous Leader, Beloved Nephew. Rest in peace Mikey, you are so loved.

Smooth Transitions 4 Teens

CAREER EDUCATION AND LIFE-SKILLS PORTFOLIO
I AM CREATING MY PERFECT LIFE

DAVID AND MYRA VANDY

www.smoothtransitions4teens.com
Two YouTube Channels on Website

BALBOA.PRESS
A DIVISION OF HAY HOUSE

Balboa Press books may be ordered through booksellers or by contacting:

Balboa Press
A Division of Hay House
1663 Liberty Drive
Bloomington, IN 47403
www.balboapress.com
844-682-1282

ISBN: 979-8-7652-4854-6 (sc)
ISBN: 979-8-7652-4855-3 (e)

Library of Congress Control Number: 2023924666

Print information available on the last page.

Balboa Press rev. date: 05/13/2024

Objectives in Smooth Transitions 4 Teens are correlated with Federal SCANS Standards (Secretary's Commission on Achieving Necessary Skills)

Name:

_____

Address:

_____

_____

Phone: Email:

_____   _____

Other information:

_____

_____

_____

SMOOTH TRANSITIONS 4 TEENS Career/Education and Life Skills Portfolio
www.smoothtransitions4teens.com

The Power of I Am

Smooth Transitions 4 Teens is written in the first
person for a very important reason.

Every time you think or say, "I am", you are coming from
a place of knowing, resolve, and

<u>what you are being now.</u>

Every time you read an objective in Smooth Transitions
4 Teens which contains the words

"I am", or "I"

you are thinking from this place of doing and being.

As you take the steps, creating your perfect life,

you are working with the power of your inner knowing.

This is where your power lies.

CONTENTS

www.smoothtransitions4teens.com
Two YouTube Channels on the website:
Smooth Transitions 4 Teens (ST4T) Videos and (Hope Journeys)

LIFE STORIES and QUOTES

INTRODUCTION

I have everything I need inside me right now to create a happy, prosperous, purposeful life. I have the ability to create the lifestyle I enjoy. Something I look forward to every day. I am taking the steps, doing what my heart leads me to do. I am building my self-confidence. I'm making a positive difference in the world. I surround myself with people who lift me up.

I Am Creating the Life I Choose - Starting Now.

As I begin, I page through all of Smooth Transitions 4 Teens.

I become familiar with its contents. This helps me get an overview, to identify possible choices I might make.

I connect with positive people around me who are willing to assist me in learning new skills, as I prepare for my future. Personal relationships and a healthy community are essential for me.

I blend the benefits of my personal relationships with the advantages of teaching myself, by checking out videos at www.smoothtransitions4teens.com. I intentionally select additional videos which I pick, to ignite my curiosity for exploring options for my future.

Videos and other electronic resources are powerful, but there is no substitute for healthy community, with people to people contact. A healthy community is where everyone acts to take care of each other.
I gain insights into the successful lives of dozens of noteworthy people through their life stories and quotes found throughout Smooth Transitions 4 Teens (ST4T).

My goals and ideas for the future may change. As circumstances change, as I experience new things, meeting new people, I make adjustments. It is very likely I will go through a period of trial and error. I may replace a career or education path, which looked good to me 6 months or a year ago with something new.

Even if I don't have any idea what my future might look like, I begin by making a commitment to myself. I face the unknown. I take the first step.

> *"Banish the doubt and carry it out."*
> Dr. Wayne W. Dyer

I start by thinking about what is important to me, what I have already accomplished, who is there for me. I take the I Am Starting Survey, continuing with 10 Steps to Creating My Perfect Life.

I focus on my Personal Objectives and those which are most timely and important to me first. I skip those which do not apply to me.

I do not have to complete all the objectives in this book. *For example,* ***if I have a job, volunteer 6 hours per month and don't intend to do an internship, I simply skip the entire internship category.***

I have many options for creating my future the way I want to. I can choose to spend more time in the beginning creating the big picture for myself, thinking about my Personal Goals. I can explore videos that interest me in the Circle of Support, Employment, Interpersonal Skills, Internships. or Volunteering categories on the Smooth Transitions 4 Teens (ST4T) video channel.

I have open space at the end of Smooth Transitions 4 Teens to help me organize as I accomplish my goals, with 24 monthly ***My Plans*** pages. At the beginning of ***My Plans***, I find references to the (Hope Journeys) Video Channel.

This channel introduces me to many critically needed Social Improvement Career Options, including Climate Crisis, Earth Stewardship and Social Justice. Watching these videos could draw me toward a potential career path.

Even if I choose a career path different from those suggestions, I can still do my part by investing in, volunteering, contributing to, or supporting in some way to a brighter, more durable future for our society and our earth. These efforts will pay ongoing dividends now and for future generations.

Additional videos on the (Hope Journeys) YouTube channel inform me about practical Community Building Choices and Positive Relationship Approaches, providing strategies to help me connect with others, help someone else, and to grow from within.

I record my information in the various categories of Smooth Transitions 4 Teens.
I am gradually creating my own Personal Portfolio.
When I go on job, internship, apprenticeship, or volunteer interviews, I take Smooth Transitions 4 Teens with me. I have everything at my fingertips to show and describe my accomplishments. I know a challenge like this takes time and effort.

I act and don't look back. I am totally worth it!
I routinely go to (ST4T) and (Hope Journeys) YouTube channel links on the website
FIRST. This helps me get started. It assists me in completing objectives in ST4T.
@
www.smoothtransitions4teens.com

I go to ***www.smoothtransitions4teens.com***

(ST4T) YouTube video channel:

10 Steps/Goal Setting/Time Management

The Strong Secret to Success

Earl Nightingale

Source: After Skool

"Learn to enjoy every minute of your life. Be happy now. Don't wait for something outside of yourself to make you happy in the future.
Think how really precious is the time you have to spend, whether it's at work or with your family. Every minute should be enjoyed and savored"
Earl Nightingale

I Am Starting Survey

I have a helper ask me these questions, if possible, and record my answers. Otherwise, I do it myself.

Date:

1. What are my hobbies and interests? What do I do in my free time?

2. What problems in my town or the world need to be fixed and how can I help solve them?

"Act in the living present."
Henry Wadsworth Longfellow

3. What is happening in the world or my town that I think is good, that I want to support? What could I do to give my support to these things or situations?

4. What am I naturally good at?

5. Do I work better by myself, with another person, with small groups of people, or in large groups?

6. Would I like to own my own business, work for a large corporation, for a small company, or...?

7. Would I like to live near where I live now, somewhere else, in another part of the country, or in another country?

8. Who loves me? Who is there for me when I need support?

9. My ideas about what I might like to do someday for my job or profession...

My helper tells a positive, descriptive story about me, using the information in my survey. If I am alone, I stand in front of a mirror, and confidently and enthusiastically tell my story to that fine person in the mirror.

"Remember always that you have not only the right to be an individual:
you have an obligation to be one. You cannot make any useful contribution in life unless you do this.
The future belongs to those who believe in the beauty of their dreams."

Eleanor Roosevelt
First Lady of the United States 1933-1945.
American politician, activist, special envoy to the President.

Dyer's Dozen
Dr. Wayne W. Dyer
Twelve Steps to Connect with Intention

1. Want more for others than you want for yourself.

2. Think from the end.
Begin to see yourself surrounded by people and the events,
and things that you would like to have.

3. Be an appreciator of your life.
Look for what is valuable rather than worthless.

4. Stay in rapport with Source Energy.
Your job is to be in a state of harmony.

5. Resistance: Every thought you have that is other than
that which you emanated from is resistance.

6. Contemplate yourself as surrounded by the conditions which you want to produce.

7. Understand the art of allowing.
Allowing means taking the path of least resistance.

8. Practice radical humility.

9. Be in a constant state of gratitude.
Be grateful for everything that shows up in your life.

10. You can never resolve a problem by condemning it.

11. Play the match game.
Always ask yourself, "Am I matched up with the field of intention"?

12. Meditate!
Make it a practice in your life. Meditation is essential because
it is your way of staying connected to source.

"When you are inspired…
you discover yourself to be a
greater person by far than you
ever dreamed yourself to be."

Dr. Wayne W. Dyer

Best-Selling Author, Highly Successful World-Renowned Motivational Speaker, and Spiritual Teacher

Born during the depression in Detroit 1940, Wayne and his big brother grew up in an orphanage, followed by a series of foster homes. His alcoholic father had walked out on his family when Wayne was one year old. His mother finally got her kids back. In his teen years Wayne at times refused to comply with school rules, in part because his mom had remarried another alcoholic who was emotionally and physically abusive to him.

From boyhood Wayne was always a person to speak up. In elementary school, when a new student came to his school and was tormented because she was Jewish, Wayne stood up for her. His classmates stopped. While he was serving in the navy in Guam, native, brown-skinned Guamanians working at the store on base were excluded from receiving the employee discount. Wayne entered a contest to respond to the injustice of this discrimination and won the $75 prize. He faced a possible court martial but stood his ground. No charges were brought against him. The policy was changed.

Author of 41 books, Dr. Dyer has been called the father of motivation. His first book, Your Erroneous Zones, published in 1976, was translated into dozens of languages. It became the #1 best-selling book of the entire decade during the 1970's.

"If you change the way you think about things, you can create whatever it is you want for yourself in life."

Wayne gave up drinking in his early years. He hosted numerous fundraisers for his beloved PBS, was married and divorced. A loving father of 8 children, he passed away at 75 of leukemia.

Dr. Wayne Dyer; a decades-long mentor, inspiration, and healing teacher for the authors of this book. Thank you, Wayne!

Source: (In Part) YouTube- The Amazing Life Story of Dr. Wayne Dyer: Faith and Inspiration: and I Can See Clearly Now; Hay House; Audio Book; Biography read by the author

10 Steps to Creating My Perfect Life

1. I make a list of what I may want to do with my future, what I want to have, what I want to be, and the kind of person I want to be.

   * I brainstorm, and let my imagination run free. I follow my heart and listen closely to my feelings. *

2. I create a picture in my mind. I picture myself already working in the career I am meant for.
   * I relax, I observe myself, as if I am watching myself in a movie.

"You must find a place inside yourself where nothing is impossible."
Dr. Deepak Chopra

10 Steps to Creating My Perfect Life

3. I See myself doing this work now. It is perfect for me!

   ** How do I feel? How am I dressed? Where am I living?

4. I think of it in the present, I think _from_ it rather than _of_ it * It already exists. *

5. I picture myself calm and relaxed, accomplishing much without strain or excessive effort.

   * I am the observer of these scenes! *

6. I am taking practical steps, accomplishing my goals. I am achieving them.

7. <u>I am feeling so fulfilled!</u>

10 Steps to Creating My Perfect Life

8. I'm receiving the rewards I have earned.
   ** I am earning $ _____ a year.

   ** My home is _____

   I CONGRATULATE myself NOW!

9. I create a vision board for myself.

   ** I cut out pictures, and phrases from magazines or other places which describe and display my vision and attach them to my vision board.
   ** I place my vision board where I see it every day.

10. <u>I write out my vision in a sentence or two</u>. I add it to my vision board.

I read and mentally rehearse my vision several times * EVERY DAY*. I record it on my phone. I do not share my vision widely. I keep my vision to myself minimizing negative outer influence.

** I modify my vision as I need to *

I go to <u>www.smoothtranstions4.com</u> (ST4T) video channel:
10 Steps to Creating My Perfect Life/ Goal Setting/ Time Management

"Man is made by his belief. As he believes, so he is."
Johann Wolfgang von Goethe

"Believe you can
and you're halfway there"
President Theodore Roosevelt

Theodore (Teddy) Roosevelt was born in 1858 to a wealthy family in New York. At the age of 46, Teddy became the youngest President of the United States until John F. Kennedy, who was 43. He dramatically expanded the power of the presidency through presidential proclamations and orders. He is most recognized as the President who fought the battle of breaking up the unchecked power of the great monopolies, using the Sherman Anti-Trust Act. He was a champion of democracy for all Americans. Teddy's love of nature and the wisdom to protect it resulted in the preservation of over 200 million acres of American wilderness.

SOURCE: https://upload.wikimedia.org/wikipedia/commons/e/eb/T_Roosevelt.jpg

As a youth, Teddy was home-schooled and sickly, but did his best to overcome through extensive exercise. He graduated from Harvard, attended but dropped out of Columbia Law School, married Alice Lee, and soon entered politics as a member of the New York Assembly. Shortly thereafter, both his wife and mother died on the same day.

Grief stricken; Theodore headed for the Badlands of North Dakota to start over. He left his young daughter with his sister. The future president's time in North Dakota and the West surely helped to shape his thinking about the value of preserving wilderness when he became president. Theodore Roosevelt was a pioneering leader in what is now considered the modern environmental movement.

Roosevelt returned to New York city in 1886, ran for mayor but lost. He married his second wife Edith, with whom he had 5 children. Teddy was appointed assistant secretary of the navy, starting in 1897. In 1898 he served in the Spanish-American war, where he led the famous capture of San Juan Hill. TR returned home a war hero and was elected governor of New York. The 1900 presidential election saw Roosevelt elected Vice-President under President William McKinley. McKinley was assassinated, elevating Theodore Roosevelt to the Presidency less than a year after the election.

Teddy ran in 1904 and won. While in office, he increased the strength of the navy, oversaw the completion of the Panama Canal, and received the Nobel Peace Prize. He vowed not to run again for the presidency.

The President was always moving, doing, and leading at a feverish pace, frequently exclaiming to others that he was 'dee-lighted'. TR was known to have eaten a dozen eggs for breakfast every day. His daughter recalled that her father talked incessantly. He always wanted to be the center of attention. "Father wanted to be the bride at every wedding and the corpse at every funeral". A visitor to the oval office came for an hourlong meeting with the President. When asked what he said to the President, he replied, "I told him my name." He never got in another word.

Roosevelt left office in 1909, only to return from his two-year African Safari to run for President again on a third-party ticket. He lost in a close race. After politics the ex-President wrote books and traveled the world. President Theodore Roosevelt died in 1919 at his Long Island estate. He was 60 years old.

SOURCE: YouTube: Theodore Roosevelt: Youngest U.S. President and Nobel Prize... Biography

"Projects that connect young people productively
with other youth and adults
Are now seen to be the foundations upon which
healthy communities can be built."

John P. Kretzmann and John McKnight

Authors and community building leaders, John, and John P.
co-wrote <u>Building Communities From the Inside Out; A Path
Toward Finding And Mobilizing A Community's Assets</u>

Professor McKnight worked for many years as a neighborhood organizer
in Chicago. He started the Center for Urban Affairs at Northwestern
University and co-founded with John Kretzmann the (ABCD) Asset
Based Community Development Institute, helping neighborhoods
become stronger by focusing upon their assets rather than deficits.
ABCD principles are now successfully employed in
dozens of countries around the world.
*Source: **<u>Building Communities From the Inside Out; A Path
Toward Finding and Mobilizing a Community's Assets</u>***

*"Here is the rub: Systems that are constructed for order cannot provide satisfaction in
domains that require a unique and personal human solution. This is not a critique of
any individual's leadership or method of operation. It is that systems have a limit by their
nature, they cannot provide prosperity or peace of mind or a life of satisfaction."*
John McKnight, The Abundant Community: Awakening the Power of Families and Neighborhoods

*See videos: I go to: smoothtransitions4teens.com (ST4T) Internships/ Volunteering, and
(Hope Journeys) video channel / Community Building Choices*

CIRCLE OF SUPPORT

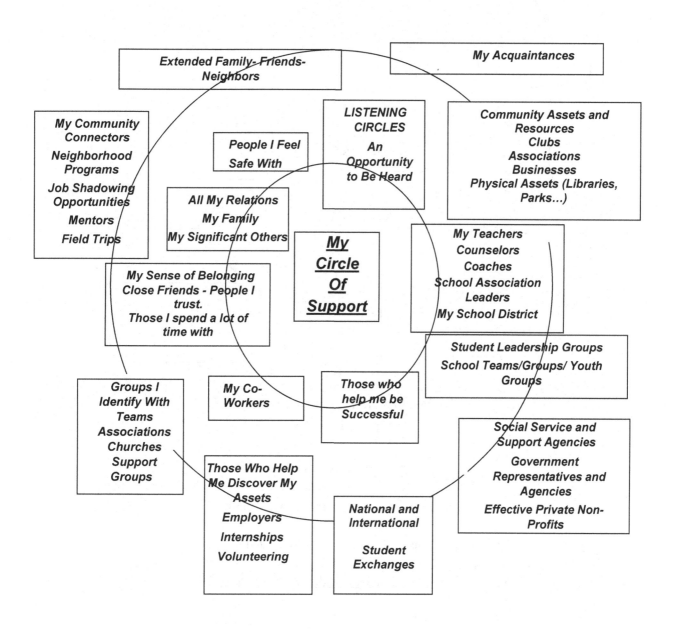

Extended Family- Friends- Neighbors

My Acquaintances

My Community Connectors
Neighborhood Programs
Job Shadowing Opportunities
Mentors
Field Trips

People I Feel Safe With

LISTENING CIRCLES
An Opportunity to Be Heard

Community Assets and Resources
Clubs
Associations
Businesses
Physical Assets (Libraries, Parks...)

All My Relations
My Family
My Significant Others

My Circle Of Support

My Teachers
Counselors
Coaches
School Association Leaders
My School District

My Sense of Belonging
Close Friends - People I trust.
Those I spend a lot of time with

Student Leadership Groups
School Teams/Groups/ Youth Groups

Groups I Identify With
Teams
Associations
Churches
Support Groups

My Co-Workers

Those who help me be Successful

Social Service and Support Agencies
Government Representatives and Agencies
Effective Private Non-Profits

Those Who Help Me Discover My Assets
Employers
Internships
Volunteering

National and International
Student Exchanges

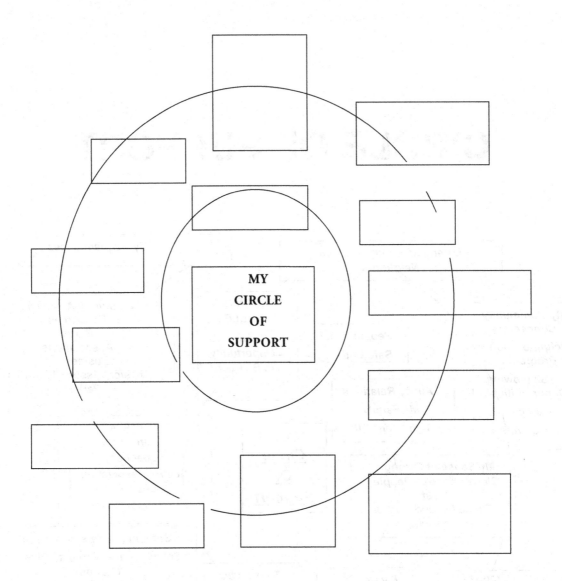

"We're wired to care for one another"
Dr. Joe Dispenza

My Circle of Support

Helps me build upon my strengths and abilities.

Facilitates my sense of belonging and connectedness to others.

Opens doors for me because <u>I am leading</u> in decisions that affect me.

Might improve relationships with my family, significant others,
and with those I choose to partner with for support.
I go to <u>www.smoothtranstions4teens.com</u> (ST4T) video channel: Circle of Support/ Future
Community Connections, and (Hope Journeys) video channel: Community Building Choices-
Circle Process

Objective # 1:

When I am looking for someone to talk to that I trust the most, when I need support, or just want somebody to listen, I call on....

"We don't accomplish anything in this world alone."
Sandra Day O'Conner- Supreme Court Justice

Objective # 2:
When I want someone to talk to about my ideas and plans for my future, I talk to...

Objective # 3
If I or someone I care about has a problem, or is in trouble, I connect with...

"Connectedness has the power to counterbalance adversity."
Dr. Bruce D. Perry

Objective # 4:

My closest supporters include: ....
I go to: www.smoothtransitions4teens.com (ST4T) video channel: Circle of Support/ Future
Community Connections.

Objective # 5:
I spend time twice a month or more with someone I admire.
I go to www.smoothtransitions4teens.com (ST4T) video channel: Circle of Support/ Future
Community Connections. I write about the qualities I admire in this person.

*When I show sincere interest in and demonstrate respect for someone who has accomplished
good things in their life by asking questions and really listening, I learn so much.
I choose to engage with the purpose of learning*

Objective # 6

I am open to joining a support group specific to an area in which I may need support. I talk to people I trust. I check online search in my local newspaper, at school, community center, church…

I go to www.smoothtransitions4teens.com (ST4T) video channel: Circle of Support/Future Community Connections.

*There are many informal groups and organizations at schools, in my neighborhood, and community, where I can find support. If appropriate, organizations such as alcoholics anonymous, substance abuse groups or mental health counseling are available.

Additional places where I can expand my circle of support might include environmental groups or sports teams such as swimming, baseball, basketball, kayaking, tennis, soccer, volleyball......*

Other options may include reading clubs, online groups, youth groups, civic clubs, travel clubs…, (See pg. 96, Creating Community – Asset Based Community Development (ABCD).

Information:

Objective # 7:

I do at least one thing each day to help others. <u>I consciously choose to accomplish this every day.</u> (See Benefits of Volunteering, pg. 212)

I go to <u>www.smoothtransitions4teens.com</u> (ST4T) video channel Internships/Volunteering and (Hope Journeys) video channel: Community Building Choices for ideas.

<u>I am creating my circle of support by what I give to others. Giving opens the way for receiving.</u> It is amazing how natural and easy this has become for me once I made it a habit.

Notes:

Objective # 8:

I seek out opportunities to actively support things I believe in. <u>I give what I need or want. I soon discover that what I am doing, and who I am being, often ends up bringing me the things I want or need. I'm not expecting something in return, I'm just allowing for whatever happens.</u>

Types of Circles

Talking
Understanding
Healing
Sentencing
Support
Community-
Building
Conflict
Reintegration
Celebration
Decision-
making

Paraphrased Source: "The Little Book of Circle Processes"
by Kay Pranis

How Circles Work

* Everyone is respected
* Everyone gets a chance to talk without being interrupted
* Everyone is equal
* All viewpoints are welcome

Circles Require

A Talking Piece- the person speaking holds the piece, handing it to the next person when finished.

Leader- monitors the time and group process but does not control decision-making.

Guidelines- promises participants make about how they will conduct themselves during the circle.

Consensus Decision-making, everyone has a say.

I go to www.smoothtransitions4teens.com (Hope Journeys) YouTube video channel: Community Building Choices

"Everyone has inside of them
A piece of good news.
The good news is that you don't know how GREAT you can be!
How much you can LOVE!
What you can ACCOMPLISH!
and
What your POTENTIAL is!"

Anne Frank
One of the Most Widely Read and Influential Authors of the
20th Century

During the holocaust of World War II, Anne was in hiding with her family in a house in Amsterdam, Holland for over two years. This young, Jewish teenager wrote <u>Anne Frank: the Diary of a Young Girl</u>. Over 30 million copies were sold and translated into over 60 languages. Anne Frank never lived to see her book published, or her 16th birthday.

The only person in Anne's family who survived the death camps of the holocaust was her father, Otto.

SOURCE: YouTube- The Life Story of Anne Frank

*Ideas * Plans * Information * Notes*

*Ideas * Plans * Information * Notes*

Longmont Mural—courtesy of City of Longmont, CO, and Gamma Acosta (artist)

EDUCATION

Homer Hickam
Nasa Rocket Engineer
True Story of a Boy from West Virginia
Chronicled in the Movie:
October Sky

I check out the fantastic accomplishments of this man. Homer came from the small town of Coalwood, West Virginia, where most boys were destined to spend their lives working in the coal mine.

After winning a national science competition for high schoolers, Hickam won a college scholarship which launched his amazing career. Homer and his high school classmates, who worked on their rocket project as a team, were known as The Rocket Boys.

I take some extra time to watch the special features at the end of the movie. Homer speaks about the importance of education, how it opened so many doors for him. It totally changed his life.

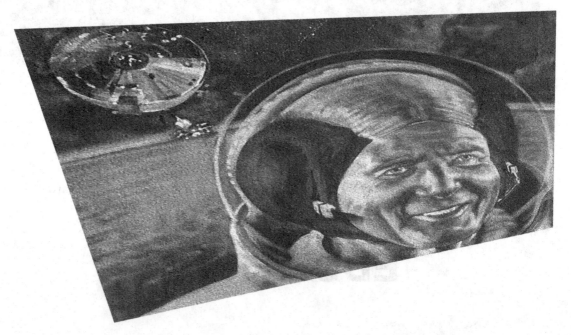

Longmont Mural—courtesy of City of Longmont, CO, and Gamma Acosta (artist)

Objective # 1:

I am seeking out alternate ways to earn high school or higher education credits.
*I talk to people I know who are doing so, plus teachers and counselors.
I go to www.smoothtransitions4teens.com (ST4T) video channel: Education, and do more research*

I earn my high school diploma or GED and obtain my transcripts.

I improve my test scores by routinely using acronyms to memorize information.
For example:
Name the 5 Great Lakes:
HOMES (Huron, Ontario, Michigan, Erie, Superior)

Information:

Objective # 2:

I am participating in educational field trips. *

These could be school organized trips to a business or community facility, or trips with family or friends. A vacation could spark my interest in a potential career or education path, or even a place I may choose to live in the future*
I go to www.smoothtransitions4teens.com (ST4T) video channel: Education.

Locations, dates, experiences:

Objective # 3

I interview professionals in areas of my educational interest.

*I initiate conversations and tell the person I'm interviewing what my interests are. I ask about what they studied or where they worked. I ask where they got their training and where they went to school. I ask about the steps they took along the way to get where they are now. I find that most people are happy to share their journey with me. I am learning so much.
I go to www.smoothtransitions4teens.com (ST4T) video channel: Education.

Experiences, names, dates, location:

Objective #4:

I do internet higher education research, (apprenticeships, vocational schools, community colleges, or universities) to find out what is the best for me right now.

*I talk to people I trust, like guidance counselors and people who have already done what I am thinking of pursuing. This helps me make informed choices. *
I go to www.smoothtransitions4teens.com (ST4T) video channel: Education.

Information:

Objective # 5:

I apply to schools and research available financial aid resources: scholarships, work study possibilities, FAFSA, (Free Application for Federal Student Aid), grants, student loans, etc.

I am doing financial aid research 18 months before I will need it, or as soon as I can. I talk to people who have already been through this process. I get help, watch online videos or find other sources. *
I go to www.smoothtransitions4teens.com (ST4T) video channel: Education.

Information:

Objective # 6:

I visit schools of my choice, (colleges, universities, apprenticeship programs community colleges, trade schools, or on the job training programs....).

*I thoroughly check out and read reviews for schools I am considering. I speak with advisors and student advisors. I make appointments ahead of time. I set up tours of the facilities, often led by current students. I talk to as many other students, trainees, or apprentices as I can to see what kind of feeling I get. I always listen to my feelings. *

I go to www.smoothtransitions4teens.com (ST4T) video channel: Education.

> "Accept *no one's definition of your life: define yourself.*"
> Robert Frost

Record information:

Objective # 7:

Below I list schools I have attended, with dates, addresses, and contact information.
I take SMOOTH TRANSITIONS 4 TEENS with me when I fill out job applications or go on an interview. I always have my education history with me to complete job applications easily

Name and Address of school:_____

_____

Phone Number: _____

Website _____

Contact Person(s): _____

Dates attended: FROM:_____TO: _____

Last Grade: _____

_____

Date of Graduation: _____

Degree or Certification Earned: _____

Awards or Recognitions: _____

_____

_____

- -

Name and Address of school:_____

_____

Phone Number: _____

Website _____

Contact Person(s): _____

Dates attended: FROM:_____ TO: _____

Last Grade: _____

Date of Graduation: _____

Degree or Certification Earned: _____

Awards or Recognitions: _____

Objective # 7 (continued):

Name and Address of school:_____

_____

Phone Number: _____

Website _____

Contact Person(s): _____

Dates attended: FROM:_____TO: _____

Last Grade: _____

_____

Date of Graduation: _____

Degree or Certification Earned: _____

Awards or Recognitions: _____

_____

- -

Name and Address of school:_____

_____

Phone Number: _____

Website _____

Contact Person(s): _____

Dates attended: FROM:_____TO: _____

Last Grade: _____

Date of Graduation: _____

Degree or Certification Earned: _____

Awards or Recognitions: _____

Objective # 7 (continued):

Name and Address of school:_____

_____

Phone Number: _____

Website _____

Contact Person(s): _____

Dates attended: FROM:_____TO: _____

Last Grade: _____

_____

Date of Graduation: _____

Degree or Certification Earned: _____

Awards or Recognitions: _____

_____

- -

Name and Address of school:_____

_____

Phone Number: _____

Website _____

Contact Person(s): _____

Dates attended: FROM:_____TO: _____

Last Grade: _____

Date of Graduation: _____

Degree or Certification Earned: _____

Awards or Recognitions: _____

Objective # 7 (continued):

Name and Address of school:_____

_____

Phone Number: _____

Website _____

Contact Person(s): _____

Dates attended: FROM:_____TO: _____

Last Grade: _____

_____

Date of Graduation: _____

Degree or Certification Earned: _____

Awards or Recognitions: _____

_____

- -

Name and Address of school:_____

_____

Phone Number: _____

Website _____

Contact Person(s): _____

Dates attended: FROM:_____TO: _____

Last Grade: _____

Date of Graduation: _____

Degree or Certification Earned: _____

Awards or Recognitions: _____

Objective # 8:

My Personal Program of Study
This may include any higher education: Vocational, Technical, On-the-Job Training, Community
College …
For numerous videos for education planning strategies, I go to www.smoothtransitions4teens.com (ST4T) video channel: Education.

YEAR 1:

GOAL 1:   Date Completed: _____

GOAL 2:   Date Completed: _____

GOAL 3:   Date Completed: _____

"I don't know that there are any short cuts to doing a good job."
*"Doing a good job, means hopefully, you gave it your best effort. It might
feel like people take short cuts to **success**, but you putting in the work
and doing a good job will teach you so much more in the long run!*

Sandra Day O'Conner - Supreme Court Justice

Objective # 8 (continued)

My Personal Program of Study

YEAR 1

	Date Begin	Date End	Course Name Course Number	Teacher Name	# Units/ Credits	Required/ Elective Enter R or E	Grade + *Grade Point Average
1st Semester							
							*GPA
2nd Semester							
							*GPA
1st Summer Session							
							*GPA
2nd Summer Session							
							*GPA

Objective # 8 (continued)

My Personal Program of Study

YEAR 2

YEAR 2: _____

<u>GOAL 1:</u>   Date Completed: _____

<u>GOAL 2:</u>   Date Completed: _____

<u>GOAL 3:</u>   Date Completed: _____

Objective # 8 (continued)

My Personal Program of Study

YEAR 2

	Date Begin	Date End	Course Name Course Number	Teacher Name	# Units/ Credits	Required/ Elective Enter R or E	Grade + *Grade Point Average
1st Semester							
							*GPA
2nd Semester							
							*GPA
1st Summer Session							
							*GPA
2nd Summer Session							
							*GPA

Objective # 8 (continued)

My Personal Program of Study

YEAR 3

YEAR 3: _____

GOAL 1:   Date Completed: _____

GOAL 2:   Date Completed: _____

GOAL 3:   Date Completed: _____

Objective # 8 (continued):

My Personal Program of Study

YEAR 3

	Date Begin	Date End	Course Name Course Number	Teacher Name	# Units/ Credits	Required/ Elective Enter R or E	Grade+ *Grade Point Average
1st Semester							
							*GPA
2nd Semester							
							*GPA
1st Summer Session							
							*GPA
2nd Summer Session							
							*GPA

Objective # 8 (continued)

My Personal Program of Study

YEAR 4

YEAR 4: _____

<u>GOAL 1:</u>   Date Completed: _____

<u>GOAL 2:</u>   Date Completed: _____

<u>GOAL 3:</u>   Date Completed: _____

Objective # 8 (continued):

My Personal Program of Study

YEAR 4

	Date Begin	Date End	Course Name Course Number	Teacher Name	# Units/ Credits	Required/ Elective Enter R or E	Grade+ *Grade Point Average
1st Semester							
							*GPA
2nd Semester							
							*GPA
1st Summer Session							
							*GPA
2nd Summer Session							
							*GPA

Objective # 8 (continued):

My Personal Program of Study

YEAR 5

School Name:

	Date Begin	Date End	Course Name Course Number	Teacher Name	# Units/ Credits	Required/ Elective Enter R or E	Grade+ *Grade Point Average
1st Semester							
							*GPA
2nd Semester							
							*GPA
1st Summer Session							
							*GPA
2nd Summer Session							
							*GPA

Objective # 8 (continued)

My Personal Program of Study

YEAR 5

YEAR 5: _____

GOAL 1:   Date Completed: _____

GOAL 2:   Date Completed: _____

GOAL 3:   Date Completed: _____

Objective # 9

If I have an interest in pursuing a career path in education as a teacher, administrator, or other education related profession, I do online video research. I also connect with those who are already working in my potential career field of interest.

I go to www.smoothtransitions4teens.com (ST4T) video channel: Education.

"Two roads diverged in the wood,
and I took the one less traveled
and that has made
all the difference"

Robert Frost

One of America's Most Widely Read and Beloved Poets: Four-Time Pulitzer Prize Winner

Robert Frost became a national celebrity. He received 40 honorary degrees and a congressional gold medal. At the age of 80 Robert Frost was invited to speak at the inauguration of John F. Kennedy. Ever the poet, passing at 89, his tombstone read,

"I had a lover's quarrel with the world."

At a speech at the dedication of the Robert Frost Library in 1963 President Kennedy remarked, "power corrupts, poetry cleanses." In his poetry Robert Frost wrote truth to power.

"Freedom lies in being bold."

Source: YouTube: Robert Frost- American Poet& Four –Time Pulitzer Prize Winner: Biography

*Ideas * Plans * Information * Notes*

*"Everything you do is
triggered by an emotion
of either desire or fear."*

Brian Tracy
Author, International Motivational Trainer of Over 5,000 Seminars

This highly successful man has led 5,000 motivational seminars for some of the top companies in the world for decades, beginning with motivational talks for young adults. He is the author of more than 80 books.

Brian had a challenging childhood due to financial instability in his family. His dad did not keep steady work. Young Brian and his three brothers had to live wearing only charity clothes. His parents often said, "We can't afford it, we have no money". He began to wonder why he could not afford 90% of the things that others could. Tracy wanted to solve this problem.

Brian started primary school with little interest in school. He soon dropped out of school, traveled through North America, took a ship to England, then France and Spain, returning eight years later. His travels continued to London, Singapore, and Malaysia. Tracy now says he has traveled to more than 80 countries thus far.

Back in Canada, Brian worked as a salesman, although he was untrained. Seeking more knowledge from experienced salesmen served him well. He became the top salesman. As a 25-year-old, Tracy rose to become vice-president of the company. Tracy helped his employer achieve the top spot in its field.

By 1981, Brian Tracy started The Phoenix Seminar, motivating young people to succeed in life. This led to the establishment of his company, Brian Tracy International in 1984, based in Vancouver, British Columbia, Canada.

Tracy's company helps clients learn the leadership skills necessary for building successful businesses. In addition to the more than 80 books he has written in his life, he has many resources for success on his YouTube channel.

In 2010, Brian was diagnosed with throat cancer and credits his faith for defeating the cancer, allowing him to return to work.

Brian Tracy wants to let others know the potential of a human. "If someone like me, who came from nothing can be a success, then why not you?

*"Stand up today and show something that you deserve. The act of taking the
first step is what separates the winners from the losers." - Brian Tracy*

Source: YouTube: Brian Tracy Inspirational Biography/ Success Story/ Next Biography

EMPLOYMENT

"Do the best you can in every task,
no matter how unimportant it may seem at the time.
No one learns more about a problem than the person at the bottom."

Sandra Day O'Conner- Supreme Court Justice

Objective # 1:

I have the necessary documents and have recorded my essential information before I look for a job.

I go to www.smoothtransitions4teens.com (ST4T) video channel: Employment/Legal Issues.

*I make sure I have my education history information, which I recorded in Education Objective #7. I take SMOOTH TRANSITIONS 4 TEENS with me when I fill out job applications or go on a job interview. I enter my information when I fill out a job application. I share what I have accomplished with the interviewer *

Social Security card

** I contact the local Social Security office in my town. They will tell me the steps for obtaining either a new or replacement social security card if I don't have one. I always protect my social security number, keeping it secret to protect me from identity theft. I don't carry my card with me.*

ID card

** I call or go online to contact the local Department of Motor Vehicles (DMV or MVD). They will tell me the steps for obtaining a state issued ID card*

My employment history and contact information for employers.

I am totally prepared by having my information recorded and right in front of me. It is recorded in Employment Objective #10 below. I set myself apart during an interview with SMOOTH TRANSITIONS 4 TEENS. I confidently show the interviewer all I have accomplished

Objective # 2:

I write my resume' and update it as I need to.
I go to www.smoothtransitions4teens.com (ST4T) video channel: Employment/Legal Issues for
tips on writing a great resume'. I ask people I trust for help.

Date I completed my resume', notes:

Objective # 3:

I search the internet for employment ideas and possibilities. I spread the word among people I know, to let them know what I am doing.
I go to www.smoothtransitions4teens.com (ST4T) video channel: Employment/Legal Issues.

I record important information only and create a file on my computer and/or phone

> *"Let us then be up and doing, with a heart for any fate, still achieving,*
> *still pursuing, learn to labor, and to wait."*

> *Henry Wadsworth Longfellow*

Objective # 4:

I obtain employment applications from the person who does the hiring, if possible.
I go to www.smoothtransitions4teens.com (ST4T) video channel: Employment/Legal Issues.

Names, contact information, etc.

Objective # 5:

I request letters of recommendation from my employer before I move on to my next job.
I go to www.smoothtransitions4teens.com (ST4T) video channel: Employment/Legal Issues.

*I'll always need letters of recommendation when I apply for a job.
I make sure I give my employers at least two weeks' notice before I leave a job.
I do my best to leave any job positively, even if I believe I was not treated well. *

I make copies of the letters I receive and keep them electronically or in my resume' folder.

Objective # 6:

I practice job interviewing.

*I rehearse out loud with a friend, or in front of a mirror.
I go to www.smoothtransitions4teens.com (ST4T) video channel: Employment/ Legal Issues to view examples of interviews.
I take that information and practice some more. I am doing great *

Notes, dates:

Objective # 7:

I participate in employment field trips by visiting potential places of employment, if possible. I go to www.smoothtransitions4teens.com (ST4T) video channel: Employment/Legal Issues.

*I talk to potential employers by myself and to people who are doing the work I am interested in, if possible.

Names, dates, locations and contact information*

Objective # 8:

When I go to job interviews, I find out as much about the employer as I can before I go. I research online and talk to anyone who may have insight into the potential employer.
I go to www.smoothtransitions4teens.com (ST4T) video channel: Employment/ Legal Issues.

*I dress well. I am prepared to tell why I believe I am the best candidate for the position. I am confident and positive.
I smile, I am engaging. And I just be myself. *

Notes, dates, locations, contact information:

Objective # 9:

I consistently practice my job maintenance skills: appearance, punctuality, accuracy, communication, and working as a team member. I go to www.smoothtransitions4teens.com (ST4T) video channel: Employment/ Legal Issues for help.

If I am going to be late, if I am sick, or will miss work for any reason, I give as much notice as possible to my employer. If I need time off from work, I ask permission well in advance. *

Notes:

Objective # 10:

I work at least part-time. My employment history is recorded below:

Start Date: _____ End Date: _____

Business Name:_____

_____

Business Address:_____

_____

_____

Phone number/website:_____

_____

Supervisor(s) name(s):_____

_____

My job title:_____

Job Description:_

_____

_____

_____

Average number of hours worked per week:_____

Starting Salary:_____Ending Salary:_____

Objective # 10 (continued):

I work at least part-time. My employment history is recorded below:

Start Date: _____ End Date: _____

Business Name:_____

_____

Business Address:_____

_____

_____

Phone number/website:_____

_____

Supervisor(s) name(s):_____

_____

My job title:_____

Job Description:_

_____

_____

_____

Average number of hours worked per week:_____

Starting Salary:_____Ending Salary:_____

Objective # 10 (continued):

I work at least part-time. My employment history is recorded below:

Start Date: _____ End Date: _____

Business Name:_____

_____

Business Address:_____

_____

_____

Phone number/website:_____

_____

Supervisor(s) name(s):_____

_____

My job title:_____

Job Description:_

_____

_____

_____

Average number of hours worked per week:_____

Starting Salary:_____Ending Salary:_____

Objective # 10 (continued):

I work at least part-time. My employment history is recorded below:

Start Date: _____ End Date: _____

Business Name:_____

_____

Business Address:_____

_____

_____

Phone number/website:_____

_____

Supervisor(s) name(s):_____

_____

My job title:_____

Job Description:_

_____

_____

_____

Average number of hours worked per week:_____

Starting Salary:_____Ending Salary:_____

Objective # 11:

I spend a day (or more) working with someone who works in a job or career I am interested in by job shadowing.

I am patient, polite, and inquisitive. I learn as much as I can about where I job shadow. I ask what is expected of me before I start

> *"The only way to be truly satisfied is to do what you believe is great work. And the only way to do great work is to love what you do."*
>
> *Steve Jobs*

Experiences:

"Your work is going to fill a large part of your life, and the
only way to be truly satisfied is to do what you believe is great work.
And the only way to do great work is to love what you do.
If you haven't found it yet, keep looking. Don't settle.
As with all matters of the heart, you'll know when you find it."

Steve Jobs
Apple Computer Co-Founder, Creative Technological Genius

Steve Jobs was born in 1955. Steve was soon given up for adoption. Jobs met Steve Wozniak in the early 70's, and by 1976 he, Steve Wozniak, and Ronald Wayne co-founded Apple Computer, Inc. Apple had a record-setting public stock offering in 1981 and made the Fortune 500 list in 1983. The first available personal computer was the Apple 2, released in 1977 by Steve Jobs' company.

The first Macintosh was not successful. Steve did correct problems with the computer but was still fired by his own company in 1985. He rebounded by creating Next, Inc. in 1986, and purchased the graphics group division of Lucasfilm. He developed it into what is now known as Pixar Animation Studios. As president of Pixar, Jobs released the wildly successful, first completely animated feature film 'Toy Story'. It earned $192 million. In 1991 Steve married Laurene Powell, and they had three children together.

Apple brought Jobs back in 1996, buying Next for $425 million and hiring Steve as an advisor. One year later he rose to the position of CEO of Apple. 2001 saw Jobs unveil IPOD, followed by Apple I-Tunes in 2003, changing the music industry forever.

Continuing his long string of successes, Disney bought Pixar for $7.4 billion from Mr. Jobs in 2006. Steve joined Disney's board and became the company's biggest shareholder. Always creating and achieving technological breakthroughs, Steve Jobs introduced the I Phone and Apple TV in 2007. He changed the company name to Apple, Inc., followed by the debut of Apple I Pad in 2010.

Steve underwent pancreatic surgery in 2004. He retired in 2011 and died of pancreatic cancer at age 56. Speaking at a commencement ceremony, Steve said *"Death is the destination we all share. Death is very likely the single best invention of life. It's life's change agent. It clears out the old to make way for the new. Remembering that you are going to die is the best way I know of thinking you have something to lose. You are already naked, there is no reason not to follow your heart."*

Source: YouTube: Who was Steve Jobs @BiographyTimeline

*Ideas * Plans * Information * Notes*

"The greatest glory in living lies not in never falling, but in rising every time we fall."
Nelson Mandela
Attorney, Racial Injustice Protestor, Prisoner, President,
Icon of Leadership and Humanity

Nelson Mandela, the first black president of South Africa, began his life herding sheep and cattle in South Africa's Eastern Cape.

As the son of a Chief, Nelson had access to the best education. At Fort Hare University, he became involved in student protests against racial injustice and inequality, which got him expelled. A very bright student, Nelson was the first in his family to attend university. He pursued the study of law.

In Johannesburg in 1941, Nelson worked in the mines and came into the African National Congress. Its purpose was to unite the country. He fought Apartheid, a system of legalized segregation, for a free and multi-racial South Africa. He opened the first black law practice defending mistreated black South Africans. He quickly became a target of the white leadership and was accused of treason for which he was later acquitted.

Martial law was imposed in 1960. Mandela employed violence to resist this. He was imprisoned in 1962 then sentenced to life in prison in 1964. Future President Nelson Mandela spent 27 years in prison for his beliefs. He was offered freedom several times if he agreed to abandon his beliefs, which he refused to do. In the late 1980's Apartheid was abandoned. By 1990, at age 71, Mandela was released from prison. In his writings from prison he said,

"I was not born with a hunger to be free; I was born free. I realized as a
young man that I was not free. My freedom was taken from me.".

Nelson Mandela was elected president in the country's first free election in 1994. He is universally revered as an icon of leadership and humanity.

Source YouTube: Nelson Mandela Biography: Life and Accomplishments; WatchMojo.com

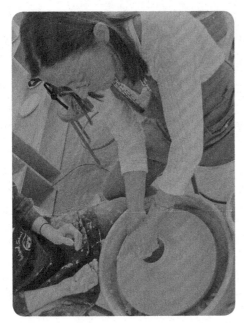

Do what you love, the money will follow.

*Ideas * Plans * Information * Notes*

FOOD AND NUTRITION

DRY MEASUREMENTS

3 teaspoons (tsp.) = 1 tablespoon (T. or Tbsp)
8 ounces (oz.) = 1 cup (c.)
16 ounces (oz.) = 1 pound (lb.)
2 cups (c.) = 16 oz. = 1 pint (pt.)

LIQUID MEASURE

8 ounces (oz.) = 1 cup (c.)
2 cups (c.) = 1 pint (pt.) = 16 ounces (oz.)
2 pints (pts.) = 1 quart (qt.) = 32 ounces (oz.)
2 quarts (qts.) = ½ gallon (gal.) = 64 ounces (oz.)
4 quarts (qts.) = 1 gallon (gal.) = 128 ounces (oz.)
60 drops (gtts) = 1 teaspoon (tsp)

LINEAR MEASURE

12 inches (in.) = 1 foot (ft.)
3 feet (ft.) = 1 yard (yd.)
5,280 feet (ft.) = 1 mile
1,760 yards = 1 mile

METRIC CONVERSIONS

1 inch = 2.54 centimeters (cm.)   1 foot = .30 meters (mt.)
1 yard = .91 meters (mt.)

1 quart (dry) = 1.1 liters (L)   1 quart (liquid) = .94 liters (L)

2.2 pounds = 1 kilogram (kg)   1 gallon (liquid) = 3.78 liters (L)

.621 miles = 1 kilometer (Km)   1 acre = .404 hectares

Objective # 1:

I plan out well-balanced meals.
I go to www.smoothtransitions4teens.com (ST4T) video channel: Food and Nutrition/ Health and Wellbeing

Basic Food Groups

Meal One:

Objective # 1 (continued):

I plan out well-balanced meals.
<u>Meal Two:</u>

<u>Meal Three:</u>

Objective # 2:

I write out my grocery list for the week: Date:

I go to www.smoothtransitions4teens.com (ST4T) video channel:
Food and Nutrition/Health and Wellbeing.

FRESH FRUITS	MEAT/POULTRY FISH / BEANS	DAIRY PRODUCTS

CANNED GOODS	SNACKS/BEVERAGES	FROZEN FOOD

PAPER PRODUCTS/ CLEANING SUPPLIES	HYGIENE PRODUCTS	OTHER

Objective # 2 (continued):

I write out my grocery list for the week: Date:

FRESH FRUITS	MEAT/POULTRY FISH / BEANS	DAIRY PRODUCTS

CANNED GOODS	SNACKS/BEVERAGES	FROZEN FOOD

PAPER PRODUCTS/ CLEANING SUPPLIES	HYGIENE PRODUCTS	OTHER

Objective # 2 (continued):

I write out my grocery list for the week: Date:

FRESH FRUITS	MEAT/POULTRY FISH / BEANS	DAIRY PRODUCTS

CANNED GOODS	SNACKS/BEVERAGES	FROZEN FOOD

PAPER PRODUCTS/ CLEANING SUPPLIES	HYGIENE PRODUCTS	OTHER

Objective # 3:

I shop for food wisely. I look for quality, price, and value.

I check store advertisements for sales and coupons to save money. I check my receipts for accuracy. I take my grocery list with me. I go with an experienced shopper to start with, if possible
I go to www.smoothtransitions4teens.com (ST4T) video channel: Food and Nutrition/Health and Wellbeing.

Dates, notes:

Objective # 4:

I am learning to cook well and safely for myself.
* I talk to people I know and ask them for help.
I go to www.smoothtransitions4teens.com (ST4T) video channel: Food and Nutrition/Health and Wellbeing and explore other videos to get ideas and to learn preparation techniques.

Dates and what I cooked:

Objective # 5:

I prepare and preserve meals ahead of time to save time and money. I freeze meals in plastic containers labeled with date and contents, to make it quick and easy when I don't have time to prepare food.
I eat better and save lots of money. I experiment with foods I normally like to eat.
I go to www.smoothtransitions4teens.com (ST4T) video channel: Food and Nutrition/Health and Wellbeing.

Notes:

Objective # 6:

I invite friends over for meals which I have prepared.
I go to www.smoothtransitions4teens.com (ST4T) video channel: Food and Nutrition/Health and Wellbeing for ideas and recipes.

What I made, date, and who came:

Objective # 7:

If I have an interest in working in food related careers, such as being a chef, nutritionist, dietician, catering, a farmer, etc., I research online whatever career path is of interest to me.

I also connect with people who are already working in my chosen field.
I go to www.smoothtransitions4teens.com (ST4T) video channel: Food and Nutrition/Health and Wellbeing.

If I am interested in careers related to food safety and food sustainability…, I go to www.smoothtransitions4teens.com: (Hope Journeys) video channel: Earth Stewardship

KITCHEN SAFETY and DISHWASHING TIPS

I fill dishpan or sink halfway with hot, soapy water, using ½ tsp of dishwashing liquid. I use water only as I need it, and do not leave the water running. My utility bill will be less, and I help my planet.

I wash dishes as I go, and rinse dirty dishes before I wash them. I rinse pots and pans between uses and fill them with water when I am finished with them. This makes an easier clean-up at the end.

I wash my cups and glasses first, then silverware, because these items touch my lips and mouth. Next are plates/bowls, cooking utensils, serving dishes, and other containers. I clean my pots and pans last.

I ALWAYS remove soap by rinsing with clean, hot water.

I DO NOT put sharp knives in my dishwater: these can cut me if I accidently grab them. I wash them separately!

When I cook raw meat, fish, poultry, or eggs, I keep the knives, dishes, cloths, and the cutting board I use, separate from other dishes, and work areas. I have one cutting board for raw meat ONLY: nothing else. I wash these dishes last, adding ½ cup of diluted bleach* water mix to dishwater. *(1 oz bleach to 1 gallon of water - I store this in a gallon jug for future use.)

I air-dry or dry dishes with a cloth and put them away.

I wipe the stove and counters as spills occur, so they don't dry onto the surface.

I empty and scrub the sink(s). I hang wet/dirty towels to prevent mildew.

I never pour grease down the sink drain. Instead, I let it cool and put all grease in a throwaway container, then put it in the trash.

I turn the stove burner down to low before I leave the kitchen. I NEVER leave the kitchen when I cook with grease (frying).

I keep baking soda nearby for grease fires. I know how to use, and where my fire extinguisher is (Home Management Objective #6).

I take out the trash (if needed) and replace the liner.

I sweep and mop my kitchen floor if it needs it. I mop when I cook with grease. A greasy floor can cause injuries. I rinse the mop with hot soapy water and hang to dry.

I rotate these responsibilities with my roommate(s) if I have one.

Mexican Food Seasoning
Tacos, Burritos…

½ c	red chili powder
2 Tbsp	dried oregano
1 tsp	onion powder
½ tsp	garlic powder
¼ tsp	dried cumin
Pinch	of salt

Directions for Both:
Blend spices together with a fork, keep in closed labeled jar, away from heat and light.

Italian Food Seasoning
Pizza, Spaghetti…….

½ c	red chili powder
2 Tbsp	dried oregano
1 tsp	onion powder
½ tsp	garlic powder
1 tsp	dried basil
Pinch	of salt

*Ideas * Plans * Information * Notes*

*Ideas * Plans * Information * Notes*

FUTURE COMMUNITY
CONNECTIONS

Creating Community
Asset Based Community Development
ABCD

We all have gifts:
HEAD – HANDS – HEART.
Encourage the gifts of others

Everyone needs to contribute their strengths, to
help create a world where they can contribute.

Share stories with others –
stories inspire change!

Identify assets in your neighborhood!

Connect with people and groups who
have skills you would like to have!

Be optimistic-
see the glass half full instead of half
empty, adding tablespoons of water as
focusing and building on assets!

People are held together by
what they care about.
Work together for common purpose!

Organize get-togethers that include food!

I go to www.smoothtransitions4teens.com
(Hope Journeys) YouTube video channel
Community Building Choices/ABCD.

Objective # 1:

I go online, search local newspapers and other sources for employment, housing, and volunteer possibilities in the location(s) I may want to live when I am on my own.
I go to www.smoothtransitions4teens.com (ST4T) video channel: Circle of Support/Future Community Connections and (Hope Journeys) video channel: Community Building Choices.

Website: _____

Website: _____

Website: _____

Website: _____

Newspaper name:_____Date: _____

Employment Possibilities:

Housing Possibilities:

Volunteer Possibilities

Objective # 2:

I research teams, groups, and organizations I might like to join in locations where I may live when I am on my own. I go to www.smoothtransitions4teens.com (ST4T) video channel: Circle of Support/ Future Community Connections. (See pg. 210, Professor John McKnight quote.)

*I am expanding my circle of support. I sometimes connect with people who are outside of groups I normally associate with. When I step out of my comfort zone, I discover things about myself and others that I've never realized before.

Dates, notes:

Objective # 3:

I visit potential volunteer sites in the location where I may live when I am on my own.
I go to www.smoothtransitions4teens.com (ST4T) video channel: Circle of Support/ Future Community Connections.

"Relationships matter. The currency for systemic change was trust.
The trust comes from forming healthy working relationships.
PEOPLE, NOT PROGRAMS, CHANGE PEOPLE"
Dr. Bruce D. Perry: (quotefancy)

I arrange to contribute a few hours each month when I am living in my new location. Unknown benefits, possibilities, recognition, new friends, and support await me

Information:

Objective # 4:

I am familiar with my future home.
I go to www.smoothtransitions4teens.com (ST4T) video channel: Circle of Support/ Future Community Connections.

*I visit places that will most likely be important to me. * I check out visitor centers, schools, possibly parks, hiking/biking trails, rec centers, churches, stores, restaurants, and my voting location. I check out banks, places where I may have a car serviced, the location of my doctor and medical facilities, and other interesting places I might like to hang out. *

Information:

Objective # 5

Things that are most important to me in my new home are:

_____

_____

_____

_____

_____

"The best preparation for TOMORROW
is doing your best TODAY"

H. Jackson Brown, Jr.
American Author of 'Life's Little Instruction Book'

1. Compliment at least 3 people every day.

4. Remember other people's birthdays.

7. Look people in the eye.

8. Say thank you a lot.

16. Be the first to say hello

17. Live beneath your means

20. Be forgiving of yourself and others

31. Buy whatever kids are selling on card tables in their front yards

38. Keep secrets

41. Don't postpone joy

43. Never give up on anybody, miracles happen every day.

44. Show respect for teachers

48. Keep a tight rein on your temper

51. Take out the garbage without being told

53. Vote

55. Stop blaming others, take responsibility for every area of your life

57. Make the best of bad situations

60. Admit your mistakes. Do not make the same mistake twice.

68. Be brave, even if you are not. Pretend to be, no one can tell the difference.

77. Don't take good health for granted

79. Don't mess with drugs and don't associate with those who do.

81. Avoid sarcastic remarks

87-88. Even if you're financially well -to-do, have your children earn and pay part of their college tuition and all their automobile insurance.

92. Choose your life's mate carefully. From this one decision will come 90% of all your happiness or misery.

112. Don't expect others to listen to your advice and ignore your example.

123. Learn to listen, opportunity sometimes knocks very softly

124. Never deprive someone of hope, it may be all that they have.

141. Give yourself an hour to cool off before responding to someone that has provoked you. If it involves something important, give yourself overnight.

152. Give people the benefit of the doubt

165. Don't waste time responding to your critics.

166. Avoid negative people

180. Do battle with prejudice and discrimination wherever you find it

197. Don't forget, a person's greatest need is to feel appreciated.

201. Don't carry a grudge

205. Loosen up, relax. Except for rare life and death matters, nothing is as important as it first seems.

"Never give up on what you really want to do.
The person with big dreams is more powerful than one with all the facts."

Source: YouTube- Life's Little Instruction Book Part 1- by H. Jackson Brown, Jr.

*Ideas * Plans * Information * Notes*

*Ideas * Plans * Information * Notes*

"Teenagers are looking for control,
*To do things the way **they** want to,*

Adults need to teach the skills with which
*Youth can **make their own choices**,*
***Track their own progress**,*
*As they prepare for **their future.***

Adults create the conditions within which
Youth live."

David Vandy

Author, Trainer, Consultant, Mentor, Community Builder,
Agent of Positive Social Change
For Youth

HEALTH AND WELL-BEING

*"The less you open your heart to others,
the more your heart suffers."*

Dr. Deepak Chopra

Objective # 1

I practice personal hygiene daily, including dental care, showering and hair care. * I choose to maintain positive mental hygiene by deciding to keep a positive attitude. *

I go to www.smoothtransitions4teens.com (ST4T) video channel: Food and Nutrition/Health and Wellbeing.

Objective # 2

I make a habit of keeping my clothes clean, laundering them weekly, at a minimum.
I go to www.smoothtransitions4teens.com (ST4T) video channel: Food and Nutrition/Health and Wellbeing.

Objective # 3

I feed myself a healthy diet. * Food is my best medicine*
I go to www.smoothtransitions4teens.com (ST4T) video channel: Food and Nutrition/Health and Wellbeing. (See Food and Nutrition, pg. 81).

Objective # 4

I educate myself about sexually transmitted disease and pregnancy prevention. * I talk to my peers and other people I trust. I do online research. I think about when and if I want to become somebody's parent. Am I ready and able to support a child? Smart choices now preserve my options for my future and will greatly benefit my kids if I choose to be a parent.
I think ahead! I go to www.smoothtransitions4teens.com (ST4T) video channel: Food and Nutrition/Health and Wellbeing, and many other online resources.

> *"It is the rare and strong person that can carry their trauma*
> *without having it spill into the next generation."*
>
> *Dr. Bruce D. Perry: (qoutefancy)*

NOTES:

Objective # 5

I have a first aid kit for my home. *I keep it available*

I go to www.smoothtransitions4teens.com (ST4T) video channel: Food and Nutrition/Health and Wellbeing.

Items, dates:

Objective # 6:

I understand how to utilize my health care benefits. I investigate services in the location I will live after I am on my own.
I know what costs I am responsible for
I go to www.smoothtransitions4teens.com (ST4T) video channel: Food and Nutrition/Health and Wellbeing.

Information:

Objective # 7:

I research potential career options in the field of health care: medicine, nursing, various hospital staffing positions, physical therapy, psychology, counseling, etc.

I go to www.smoothtransitions4teens.com (ST4T) video channel: Food and Nutrition/Health and Wellbeing, in addition to other online resources.

Objective # 8

I visit the community hospital and/or clinic locations I will use.

I investigate and know how to utilize my local emergency services. * I <u>save emergency numbers in my phone</u>. I know the route to the emergency room. I will know how to get there for myself or for someone I am helping, in case it is ever needed *

Names, addresses and phone numbers:

Objective # 9:

I check out counseling services if I think I can benefit from counseling. * I do online research and thoroughly check reviews. I make sure I am totally comfortable with any choice I may make and don't settle for anything less. *

*"Two things we can control: our attitude and our effort.
Live less out of habit and more out of intent."*

Tim Fletcher (complex trauma and addictions therapist)
YouTube: 60 Characteristics of Complex Trauma- Golden Nuggets: Helpful Perspectives

I go to (ST4T) video channel: Food and Nutrition/ <u>Health and Wellbeing</u>.

Information:

Objective # 10:

I may join a support group specific to an area in which I may want support or need assistance. I talk to people I trust. I do research.

* Online options *
Information:

Relationships matter.
The currency for systemic change is trust.
The trust comes through forming healthy, working relationships.

Dr. Bruce Perry
(quotefancy)

"The moment one definitely commits oneself, then Providence moves too.
All sorts of things occur to help one that would
never otherwise have occurred…
Unforeseen incidents, meetings, and material assistance,
which no man could have dreamed would have come his way."

"Things which matter most must never be at the
mercy of things which matter least."

Johann Wolfgang von Goethe
Writer, playwright, poet, genius of German literature

Source: YouTube- Johann Wolfgang von Goethe Life Story: Short Biographies

*Ideas * Plans * Information * Notes*

"The battles that count aren't the ones for gold medals.
The struggles within yourself-
the invisible battles inside all of us-
that's where it's at."

Jesse Owens

Olympics Star, Motivational Speaker, Goodwill Ambassador, Personnel
Director, Medal of Freedom Winner, Track and Field Hall of Famer…

Best known for winning <u>4 Gold Medals at the 1936 Olympics in Berlin, Germany</u>, Jesse Owens accomplished so many things beyond these athletic victories. It is an amazing story to hear. <u>He broke records,</u> took on segregation and stood up to one of the world's most evil dictators.

Born in 1913 in Oakville, Alabama, Jesse was the grandson of slaves and the son of sharecroppers. JC, as he was known, was the youngest of 10 children and worked alongside his parents in the cotton fields. His parents always put food on the table. When Jesse was 9, his parents moved to Cleveland, Ohio, in search of a better life, and to escape racist violence common in Alabama. Homelife was tough, with his dad and brothers out of work. Jesse had a son at the age of 18. He remained together with his wife until his death in 1980.

Jesse always loved running and <u>worked numerous after school jobs to support his family while also running track.</u> Owens was setting records as a high school senior and tried out for the 1932 Olympics. He <u>starred in track at Ohio State</u>, working part-time jobs while earning his degree. Named the Buckeye Bullet, Owens was the <u>first black captain of the athletic team</u>. Moreover, Jesse was not allowed to stay in the team hotel when they traveled. He had to stay in a boarding house instead of a dorm. Even the showers were segregated. In 2001, <u>Ohio State named their track stadium after Jesse Owens.</u>

The accomplishments of this amazing man continued. Jesse broke multiple track records, worked unpaid for the US Olympic committee to raise funds, and sold sporting goods. He worked as head of personnel for black workers at Ford Motor Co, toured with the Harlem Globetrotters, started a PR firm, and became a motivational speaker. Owens served as Secretary for the Illinois Youth Commission, was appointed to the US Olympics board of directors and was goodwill ambassador for US Sports. Owens received numerous endorsements. He was inducted into the Track and Field Hall of Fame and was awarded the Presidential Medal of Freedom.

This remarkable man overcame many personal battles within himself. Upon his retirement from athletics, Jesse started smoking a pack of cigarettes per day for 35 years. Sadly, he died of lung cancer at age 66.

SOURCE: YouTube- The Crazy Real-Life Story of Jesse Owens

*Ideas * Plans * Information * Notes*

*Ideas * Plans * Information * Notes*

HOME MANAGEMENT

*"Your home should tell the story of
who you are and be a
collection of what you love."*

Nate Berkus

Nationally recognized interior designer and home renovator

Oprah Winfrey favorite Nate Berkus is highly sought after for his excellent work, in part because of how he has overcome tragedy in his lifetime.

Born in Orange County, California in 1971, Nate Berkus went into interior design right out of high school. Nate then interned at Sotheby's in Chicago and worked as an intern in Paris. He went on to Lake Forest College in Chicago, earning degrees in French and Sociology. Nate Berkus Associates opened in 1995. Berkus has won many awards and commendations since that time.

Nate created his own interior design company in Chicago and has made regular appearances on the Oprah Winfrey Show. Tragically his partner Fernando died in a tsunami in 2005; Nate survived. The story galvanized Oprah's audience, inundating him with thousands of emails and letters.

People from all over the country felt a connection with Nate because of his loss. Thousands of people wanted to hear his story of the terror of surviving a tsunami and how he lost his husband. So many people came to know this man because of his frequent appearances with Oprah.

Nate and his new husband Jeremiah Brent have two children. Both men are interior designers. They are very well known and have a large YouTube following. Their hit TV show 'Nate and Jeremiah by Design' displays how they deal with the challenges of raising children, while helping homeowners turn difficult renovations into dream homes.

"You will enrich your life immeasurably if you approach life with a sense of wonder and discovery, and always challenge yourself to try new things."

SOURCE: YouTube- Nate Berkus Biography: Celebrity Posters
YouTube- Having More Kids- Rachel Ray Show
YouTube- Nate Berkus and Jeremiah Brent on their TLC Show: Build Series

Objective # 1: Date(s):

I learn about my community housing resources online, in newspapers, on school bulletin boards, or from someone I know.
I go to www.smoothtransitions4teens.com (ST4T) video channel: Home Management

Information:

Objective# 2:
I decide where I want to live and list the Positives and Negatives*
I go to www.smoothtransitions4teens.com (ST4T) video channel: Home Management.

Positives_____Negatives

Objective # 3:

I research housing/rental websites and newspaper classified ads.
I go to www.smoothtransitions4teens.com (ST4T) video channel: Home Management.

I check out several neighborhoods. I talk to friends and relatives and make sure I know what I can afford
I go to * Home Management Objective # 7 below, Figuring my housing costs*

Objective # 4:

I look for a place to live well before I need it.

I know what is included in rental agreements I may sign. I talk to potential future neighbors if they are out and about and ask them what the neighborhood is like. I shop around and compare
I go to www.smoothtransitions4teens.com (ST4T) video channel: Home Management.

Notes:

Objective # 5:

I ask questions. I know my landlord's and my responsibilities - *I ask for a copy of the lease. I read it and consult with someone I trust before I sign anything. I take my time and shop around. I go to www.smoothtransitions4teens.com (ST4T) video channel: Home Management.

Objective # 6:

I practice basic home repairs where I am living now. *I ask someone to help me. I have a basic tool kit so I can take care of minor home repairs on my own. I check out YouTube for the specific repair I am doing.

Date:
Tasks:

<table>
<tr><td>

How to Use a Fire Extinguisher
PASS
PULL, AIM, SQUEEZE, SWEEP

Pull the pin between the handles.

Aim the hose or nozzle at the base of the fire, leaving 6-10 feet between you and the fire.

Squeeze the fire extinguisher handle.

Sweep the extinguishing hose or nozzle from side to side to cover the base of the fire.

</td></tr>
</table>

Objective # 7:   Date(s):_____

I figure my housing costs (including utilities, deposits, renter's insurance, furnishings) <u>before</u> I sign a lease. *I may be required to pay first and last months' rent up front or a substantial deposit. <u>Utilities usually require a deposit before starting service unless</u> <u>utilities are included in my rent</u>* I go to <u>www.smoothtransitions4teens.com</u> (ST4T) video channel: Home Management.

MY TOTAL PERSONAL HOUSING COSTS

<u>First Month</u>   <u>Every Month</u>

RENT: RENT:

Electric: Electric:

Water: Water:

Gas: Gas:

Phone: Phone:

Cable: Cable:

SECURITY DEPOSIT:

OTHER DEPOSIT:
(Phone, electric, gas, water)

RENTER'S   RENTERS'
INSURANCE: INSURANCE
(optional)   (optional)

FURNITURE:

KITCHEN SUPPLIES:

OTHER   OTHER
EXPENSES: EXPENSES:

TOTAL:_____   TOTAL:_____

Objective # 7 (continued):   Date(s): _____

I figure my housing costs (including utilities, deposits, renter's insurance, furnishings) <u>before</u> I sign a lease. *I may be required to pay first and last months' rent up front or a substantial deposit. <u>Utilities usually require a deposit before starting service unless</u> utilities are included in my rent* I go to <u>www.smoothtransitions4teens.com</u> (ST4T) video channel: Home Management.

MY TOTAL PERSONAL HOUSING COSTS

<u>First Month</u>   <u>Every Month</u>

RENT: RENT:
Electric: Electric:
Water: Water:
Gas: Gas:
Phone: Phone:

Cable: Cable:

SECURITY DEPOSIT:

OTHER DEPOSIT:
(Phone, electric, gas, water)

RENTERS'   RENTERS'
INSURANCE: INSURANCE
(optional)   (optional)

FURNITURE:

KITCHEN SUPPLIES:

OTHER   OTHER
EXPENSES: EXPENSES:

TOTAL:_____   TOTAL:_____

Objective # 8:   Date(s):_____

I think through and write out how I will maintain my home <u>WITHOUT</u> roommates, including responsibilities, costs, etc.
I go to <u>www.smoothtransitions4teens.com</u> (ST4T) video channel: Home Management.

HOW I WILL MAINTAIN MY HOME <u>WITHOUT</u> ROOMMATES

<u>My Responsibilities:</u>

Objective # 8 (continued):   Date(s): _____

I think through and write out how I will maintain my home <u>WITHOUT</u> roommates, including responsibilities, costs, etc.
I go to www.smoothtransitions4teens.com (ST4T) video channel: Home Management.

HOW I WILL MAINTAIN MY HOME <u>WITHOUT</u> ROOMMATES

<u>My Costs:</u>

Beginning   Monthly   Other

_____   _____   _____

TOTALS

Objective # 8 (continued):   Date(s):_____

I think through and write out how I will maintain my home <u>WITH</u> roommates, including division of responsibilities, costs, etc.

I go to <u>www.smoothtransitions4teens.com</u> (ST4T) video channel: Home Management.

HOW I WILL MAINTAIN MY HOME <u>WITH</u> ROOMMATES

My Responsibilities:	My Roommate's Responsibilities

Objective # 8 (continued):   Date(s): _____

I think through and write out how I will maintain my home <u>WITH</u> roommates, including division of responsibilities, costs, etc.

I go to www.smoothtransitions4teens.com (ST4T) video channel: Home Management.

HOW I WILL MAINTAIN MY HOME <u>WITH</u> ROOMMATES

My Costs:			My Roommate's Costs		
Beginning	Monthly	Other	Beginning	Monthly	Other

TOTALS

Objective # 9:

I choose my roommates wisely:
*We write out and agree upon house rules and responsibilities including costs - before moving in together.
Every roommate signs the agreement*
We go to www.smoothtransitions4teens.com (ST4T) video channel: Home Management and (Hope Journeys) video channel: Community Building Choices and Positive Relationship Approaches for creating agreements positively and peacefully.

HOUSE RULES AND RESPONSIBILITIES: I (we) agree to abide by the following house rules and rotate chores to share responsibilities equally:

CHORES AND RESPONSIBILITIES	NAME	NAME
Kitchen:		
Floors:		
Trash:		
Laundry:		
Other:		

EXPENSES:

Rent:		
Utilities:		
Deposits:		
Food/Groceries:		
Other:		
Totals:		

OTHER:
Guests
Pets

SIGNATURE:_____   _____

DATE: _____   _____

Objective # 9 (continued):

I choose my roommates wisely:
*We write out and agree upon house rules and responsibilities including costs - before moving in together.
Every roommate signs the agreement*
We go to www.smoothtransitions4teens.com (ST4T) video channel: Home Management and (Hope Journeys) video channel: Community Building Choices and Positive Relationship Approaches for creating agreements positively and peacefully.

HOUSE RULES AND RESPONSIBILITIES: I (we) agree to abide by the following house rules and rotate chores to share responsibilities equally:

CHORES AND RESPONSIBILITIES	NAME	NAME
Kitchen:		
Floors:		
Trash:		
Laundry:		
Other:		

EXPENSES:

Rent:		
Utilities:		
Deposits:		
Food/Groceries:		
Other:		
Totals: _____		

OTHER:
Guests
Pets

SIGNATURE:_____   _____

DATE: _____   _____

Objective # 10:   Date(s):_____

I visit my neighborhood stores and investigate public transit that I may use in the location I will live after I am on my own.

I have access to public transit schedules if needed. I <u>sign up for grocery store discount cards, or apps to save money on my grocery bill</u>

Objective # 11:   Date(s):_____
I furnish my kitchen and home inexpensively and practically.
I go to yard sales, thrift shops, etc., to save money on things I need. I keep any receipts in my file box
I go to www.smoothtransitions4teens.com (ST4T) video channel: Home Management for ideas.

Objective # 12:   Date(s):_____

I create an electronic file and/or an alphabetically organized file box for my regular monthly bills.

* I keep and file receipts alphabetically for future reference.
I go to www.smoothtransitions4teens.com (ST4T) video channel: Home Management.

Reminders:

*I record the date, my check number and the amount paid on the portion I keep on every (paper) bill I pay. I clean my house once a week and share the work evenly if I have roommates.

I file my bills as soon as I write them out and keep them for my records. If I pay online, I check my deductions and balances at least twice a month. <u>If I have any questions or problems with my balance, I call my bank and get help</u>

Objective # 13:

I check out career options in real estate, property management…. if I have an interest.

I go to www.smoothtransitions4teens.com (ST4T) video channel: Home Management.

*Ideas * Plans * Information * Notes*

*"If we did all the things we are capable of,
we would literally astound ourselves."*

Thomas A. Edison

If you enjoy music or watching movies, or spending half your life in the dark, there is someone you should thank, Thomas Alva Edison.

THIS GREAT THINKER HAD 1093 PATENTS FOR HIS LIFE-IMPROVING INVENTIONS

Thomas was the youngest of 7 children. He came into this world in 1847, growing up in Milan, Ohio until he was 7. From his new home in Port Huron, young Alva was taught at home by his mother after recovering from scarlet fever and failing to thrive at school. Thomas may have been suffering from hearing loss due to the scarlet fever.

HIS MOM TOLD HIM THE SCHOOL SAID HE WAS SO SMART THAT THE SCHOOL DID NOT HAVE ANYONE CAPABLE OF TEACHING HIM

Thomas' teacher had actually made some very negative comments in a note to his mother about Thomas' inability to learn. After his mom died Thomas went through her papers and found the original note from the teacher.

The Edison home had a well-stocked library. Little Alva was allowed to have a laboratory in the basement where he worked his way through a book of experiments. At 12, Thomas began working for a railroad company. He published a newspaper, The Weekly Herald on board the train. His time on the train came to an abrupt end when his laboratory on the train caught fire.

Learning about telegraphs while working on trains, he invented his own and became a travelling telegraph operator. His voracious appetite for reading about science and technology continued in earnest.

HIS FIRST PATENT WAS FOR AN AUTOMATIC VOTE COUNTING MACHINE

Thomas and Mary Stillwell married when he was 24. The couple had six children naming their first 2 children Dot and Dash because of their telegraph loving father.

During this time some of Edison's inventions included * STOCK TICKERS, FIRE ALARMS * and a way to send telegraph messages at the same time on a single wire, called the double transmitter. His work earned him $40,000 from the Western Union Company in return for his many contributions to telegraph technology.

This $40,000, a small fortune in those days, allowed him to open his now famous laboratory in Menlo Park, New Jersey in 1876. He employed many assistants. The men worked all day and into the night.

"I THINK WORK IS THE GREATEST FUN."

Within a year Edison received a patent for the phonograph which made him world famous, earning him the name of The Wizard of Menlo Park.

* THE DAWN OF THE ELECTRIC LIGHT BULB *

soon followed, which many worked on. Edison and another inventor simultaneously found a way to develop a bulb which would burn longer making it commercially viable.
To get electricity into people's homes Edison invented power stations and laid underground wires to carry electricity to those homes.

By 1894 Thomas found a way to combine AUDIO AND VIDEO AT THE SAME TIME * MOVIES *

This great thinker came from humble beginnings, failed in traditional school, and was hard of hearing. He left this earth in 1931. Thomas Alva Edison changed the world for the better.

"Everything comes to him who hustles while he waits. <u>Discontent is the first necessity of progress.</u> I never did a day's work in my life; it was all fun."

"GENIUS IS ONE PERCENT INSPIRATION AND 99 PERCENT PERSPIRATION"

Source: YouTube: Who is Thomas Edison? Biography of Thomas Edison: Socratia

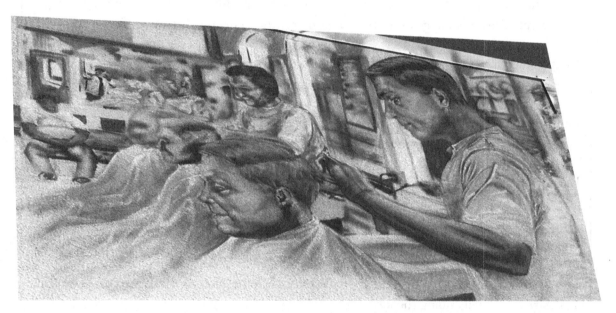

Longmont Mural—courtesy of City of Longmont, CO, and Gamma Acosta (artist)

INTERNSHIPS

BENEFITS OF INTERNSHIPS OR APPRENTICESHIPS

I gain work experience- Internships/Apprenticeships give me the opportunity to gain real-world experience and develop valuable skills before I commit to a course of study or potential career.

I add practical experience to my resume- A strong resume with real-world experience will give me a competitive advantage over other candidates when I'm applying for work.

I experience a variety of work cultures- As an intern or apprentice, I gain insights and experience working as an employee, interacting with supervisors and other co-workers.

I improve my time management skills- Internships/ Apprenticeships help me complete routine expectations, tasks and projects in a timely fashion as required.

I learn about a potential career choice or job before committing to it- Internships/Apprenticeships give me the opportunity to better determine if this specific work is the right fit for me. For example, I'll learn the time requirements, salary, benefits, responsibilities, stress level, opportunities for advancement, and more.

I boost my confidence- Internships/Apprenticeships help me gain confidence in the workplace as I learn by actually doing the job.

I may identify a specialty- If I'm engaged in a generalized field of work or study, an internship/ apprenticeship may help me specialize or change my career path.

I may find a mentor- From the connections I build as an intern/ apprentice, I may find a professional who's willing to share insights, to mentor or guide me along my career path.

I could secure a job offer- By demonstrating my skills and producing positive results in an internship/apprenticeship, I could receive a job offer, or the promise of a job after graduation or completion of other work requirements.

I go to: www.smoothtransitions4teens.com (ST4T) video channel: Internships/Volunteering

Objective # 1:

I Research Internship <u>possibilities</u>. * I check out more than one potential career before I commit to a career or education plan.

INTERNSHIP POSSIBILITY

Start Date: _____   End Date: _____

I go to <u>www.smoothtransitions4teens.com</u> (ST4T) video channel: Internships/Volunteering and (Hope Journeys) video channel playlists of my choice,
to explore social improvement career possibilities.

Business Name:

Business Address:

Telephone number/website:

Supervisor(s) name(s):

Referred by:

My Internship Title:

Description of Internship:

Average number of hours to be worked per week:

Stipends or Wages:

Objective # 1 (continued):

I Research Internship possibilities. * I check out more than one potential career before I commit to a career or education plan.

INTERNSHIP POSSIBILITY

Start Date: _____   End Date: _____

I go to www.smoothtransitions4teens.com (ST4T) video channel: Internships/Volunteering and (Hope Journeys) video channel playlists of my choice,
to explore social improvement career possibilities.

Business Name:

Business Address:

Telephone number/website:

Supervisor(s) name(s):

Referred by:

My Internship Title:

Description of Internship:

Average number of hours to be worked per week:

Stipends or Wages:

Objective # 2:

I participate in Internship Placement <u>Field Trips</u>. *I try out several possibilities*

INTERNSHIP FIELD TRIP

Date: _____

I go to <u>www.smoothtransitions4teens.com</u> (ST4T) video channel: Internships/Volunteering
and (Hope Journeys) video channel playlists of my choice,
to explore social improvement career possibilities.

Business Name:

Business Address:

Telephone number/website:

Contact Person within Organization:

Field Trip Coordinator Information:

Potential Internship Title:

Description of Internship:

Average number of hours to be worked per week:

Stipends or Wages:

Objective # 2 (continued):

I participate in Internship Placement <u>Field Trips</u>. *I try out several possibilities*

INTERNSHIP FIELD TRIP

Date: _____

Business Name:

Business Address:

Telephone number/website:

Contact Person within Organization:

Field Trip Coordinator Information:

Potential Internship Title:

Description of Internship:

Average number of hours to be worked per week:

Stipends or Wages:

Objective # 3:

I go on <u>Internship Placement Interviews.</u>

Completing more than one internship will help me be much more informed when making career decisions. <u>I prepare for an Internship Placement Interview just as I would prepare for a regular job interview</u>. I research the organization and internship for which I am applying. I am prepared to tell them why they should pick me over other applicants*

I go to <u>www.smoothtransitions4teens.com</u> (ST4T) video channel: Internships/Volunteering.

"If someone like me, who came from nothing can be a success, then why not you?"
Brian Tracy

Internship Interviews

Date: _____

Business Name:

Business Address:

Telephone number/website:

Supervisor/Interviewer name:

My Internship Title:

Description of Internship:

Average number of hours to be worked per week:

Stipends or Wages:

Objective # 3 (continued):

I go on <u>Internship Placement Interviews</u>. * <u>I take SMOOTH TRANSITIONS 4 TEENS with me when I fill out an application or interview for an internship.</u> All the information I will need will be at my fingertips. I use SMOOTH TRANSITIONS 4 TEENS as <u>my portfolio during the interview to showcase the things I have been working on</u>*

Record information:

Internship Interviews

Date: _____

Business Name:

Business Address:

Telephone number/website:

Supervisor/Interviewer name:

My Internship Title:

Description of Internship:

Average number of hours to be worked per week:

Stipends or Wages:

Objective # 4:

I practice my internship maintenance skills: my appearance, punctuality, accuracy, working as a team member. *I consistently display excellent employment skills*

I go to www.smoothtransitions4teens.com (ST4T) video channel: Internships/Volunteering.

Objective # 5:

I successfully complete an internship. *Working as an intern can definitely help me get a paid position in the future. <u>Many employers look for or require potential employees to have internship experience and sometimes hire successful interns as paid employees*</u> I intend to be one of those.

I go to www.smoothtransitions4teens.com (ST4T) video channel: Internships/Volunteering.

INTERNSHIP

Start Date: _____   End Date: _____

Business Name:

My experiences:

Objective # 5:

I successfully complete an internship. *Internships are often considered a big boost if, or when, I apply for certain higher education opportunities*

I go to www.smoothtransitions4teens.com (ST4T) video channel: Internships/Volunteering.

INTERNSHIP

Start Date: _____   End Date: _____

Business Name:

My experiences:

Objective # 6:

I meet people with experience in my internship field of interest. *I ask around. <u>I can learn a lot by speaking with someone who has already interned or apprenticed for an organization</u>*

I go to <u>www.smoothtransitions4teens.com</u> ST4T video channel: Internships/Volunteering and (Hope Journeys) video channel playlists of my choice.

NAME: DATE: _____

ADDRESS:

TELEPHONE NUMBER:

EMAIL/SOCIAL MEDIA:

RELATIONSHIP:

EXPERIENCES:

NAME: DATE: _____

ADDRESS:

TELEPHONE NUMBER:

EMAIL/SOCIAL MEDIA:

RELATIONSHIP:

EXPERIENCES:

Objective # 6 (continued):

I meet people with experience in my internship field of interest.

Record information:

NAME: DATE: _____

ADDRESS:

TELEPHONE NUMBER:

EMAIL/SOCIAL MEDIA:

RELATIONSHIP:

EXPERIENCES:

NAME: DATE: _____

ADDRESS:

TELEPHONE NUMBER:

EMAIL/SOCIAL MEDIA:

RELATIONSHIP:

EXPERIENCES:

*"What lies behind you and what lies in front of you
pales in comparison to what lies inside of you."*

Ralph Waldo Emerson
Known as the Father of American Literature.

Emerson penned several essays in the mid-19th century that fundamentally changed the way America saw its cultural and artistic possibilities.

Born in 1803, the son of a Boston preacher, Ralph went to Harvard, then on to Harvard Divinity School. He was ordained in 1829 and married that same year. His wife died just two years later. Emerson embarked on a trip to Europe. There he understood that nature is in us, a part of us.

"If great men can be so ordinary, why should not ordinary men be great."

Emerson believed that man and nature are one, that everyone can recognize they are a uniquely significant human being.

Ralph returned to America, became a lecturer, remarried, and had several children. His central belief was in being self-reliant rather than living in a way that others think we should; that there is a divine spark in each of us. "We can rebuild ourselves," he declared.

What is Success

*"To laugh often and much,
To win the respect of intelligent people
And the Affection of Children;
To earn the appreciation of honest critics
And endure the betrayal of false friends;
To appreciate beauty,
To find the best in others,
To leave the world a bit better,
Whether by a healthy child, A garden patch,
Or a redeemed social condition.
To know even one life
Has breathed easier.
This is to have succeeded."*

SOURCE: YouTube- What is Success? - Ralph Waldo Emerson, RedFrostMotivation

Embrace Conflict as a Source of Growth and Transformation
Conflict can come from a variety of sources:

1. GOALS- Conflict can happen as a result of conflicting goals or priorities. It can also happen when there is a lack of shared goals.

2. PERSONALITY CONFLICTS- Personality conflicts are a common cause of conflict. Sometimes there is no chemistry, or you haven't figured out an effective way to click with somebody.

3. SCARCE RESOURCES- Conflict can happen when you're competing over scarce resources.

4. STYLES- People have different styles. Your thinking style or communication style might conflict with somebody else's thinking style or their communication style. The good news is that conflicts in styles are easy to adapt to when you know how.

5. VALUES- Sometimes you will find conflict in values. The challenge here is that values are core. Adapting with styles is one thing, but dealing with conflicting values is another. That's why a particular business, group, or culture may not be a good fit for you. It's also why "birds of a feather flock together" and why "opposites attract, but similarities bind."

By embracing conflict as a part of life, you can make the most of each situation and use it as a learning opportunity or a leadership opportunity.
You can also use it as an opportunity to transform the situation into something better.

SOURCE: New Mexico Prevention, Response and Resiliency Program- NM Public Education Department- Safe and Healthy Schools Bureau Home - Prevention, Response & Resiliency (nmprrp.com)

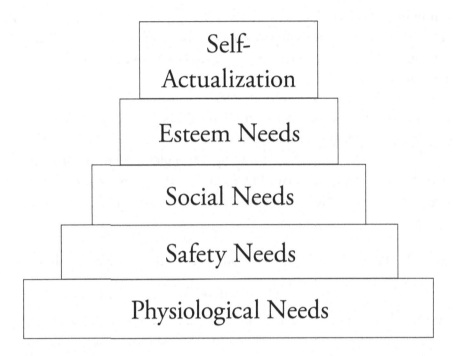

Maslow's Hierarchy
of Needs

INTERPERSONAL SKILLS

*"If your only tool is a hammer
you will see every problem
as a nail."*

Abraham Harold Maslow
World Famous American Psychologist

Son of Jewish immigrants from Russia, Abraham Maslow was born in 1908 in Brooklyn, New York. He wrote, "I was a little Jewish boy in a non-Jewish neighborhood. It was a little like being the first negro enrolled in an all-white school. I was isolated and unhappy. I grew up in libraries, among books, without friends".

His alcoholic father and unloving mother viciously attacked young Abraham's physical appearance, calling him ugly and stupid. He internalized these attacks, believing he was ugly and repulsive. Abraham avoided boarding the subway, thinking he would burden the other passengers with his appearance. Sadly, he once found two kittens and brought them home. His mother smashed their heads against the wall, killing them both, right in front of him. She even kept a lock on the refrigerator door.

Abraham married his first cousin Bertha in 1938. They were longtime sweethearts and had two daughters.

Maslow tried several colleges after high school, settled on the study of psychology and earned his PhD in 1934 from the University of Wisconsin. Dr. Maslow taught full time at Brooklyn College from 1937-1951.

Abraham suffered a heart attack in 1947 and took his family to California, returning to Brooklyn College in 1949. By 1951, he secured the chairmanship of the Psychology Department at Brandeis University.

1966 saw Dr. Maslow assume the position of president of the American Psychological Association. He retired from teaching in 1968 and died of a heart attack at 62 years of age.

Dr. Abraham Maslow is world famous for developing his <u>hierarchy of needs theory,</u> including physical, social, emotional, intellectual, and aesthetic. Most focused upon is one's ability to reach one's full potential and become all he or she is capable of, called <u>Self-Actualization</u>.

Source: YouTube -Abraham Harold Maslow; Wewantcookies8156

Longmont Mural—courtesy of City of Longmont, CO, and Gamma Acosta (artist)

"What is necessary to change a person is to change his awareness of himself."

"The ability to be in the present moment is a major component of mental wellness."

"What a man can be, he must be."

Abraham Maslow

"Self-actualizing people; those who have come to a level of high maturation, health, and self- fulfillment *have so much to teach us* that sometimes they seem almost like a *different* breed of human beings."

Objective # 1:

I think about what my needs are and how to get them met.

* I set aside some quiet time for myself to look within. I watch YouTube and other videos featuring speakers that I admire about this topic*

I go to www.smoothtransitions4teens.com (ST4T) video channel: Interpersonal Skills/Personal Objectives.

My Need	How I will get my need met.

1.

2.

```
Habits of Successful People

Meditate
Exercise
Wake up early
Consistent good sleep
Read
Pray- take time to get quiet-
take time to think
Journal
Be grateful
Review/Set priorities for your day

Source: YouTube-Tim Fletcher
Re-parenting- Part 23-Habits
```

Objective # 1:

I think about what my needs are and how to get them met.

*I take some quiet time to think; I take my time, go within, <u>am honest with myself and</u> <u>decide how I can improve.</u> I go to <u>www.smoothtransitions4teens.com</u> (ST4T) video channel Interpersonal Skills/Personal Objectives.

I go to <u>www.smoothtransitions4teens.com</u> (ST4T) video channel: Interpersonal Skills/Personal Objectives.

My Need	How I will get my need met.

3.

4.

"If I find 10,000 ways something doesn't work, I haven't failed. I am not discouraged, because every wrong attempt discarded is often a step forward."

Thomas Edison

Objective # 2:   Date(s): _____

I commit to respecting the needs of others. I talk to a trusted friend about this subject.

I think about how I want others to respect me and my needs. I treat others the way I want to be treated. <u>Sometimes people will look out for me and what I need because they observe me acting toward others in that way</u>

I go to <u>www.smoothtransitions4teens.com</u> (ST4T) video channel: Interpersonal Skills/Personal Objectives and (Hope Journeys) video channel: Community Building Choices and Positive Relationship Approaches.
Notes:

Objective # 3:

I practice asserting myself. I stand up for <u>my rights positively.</u> I assume <u>my</u> <u>responsibilities.</u> I take responsibility for myself first. *I speak in <u>I statements</u> as much as possible rather than blaming people, even if I believe I am right. How my message is sent is more important than how it is received*
I go to <u>www.smoothtransitions4teens.com</u> (ST4T) video channel: Interpersonal Skills/Personal Objectives and (Hope Journeys) video channel: Community Building Choices and Positive Relationship Approaches.
.

"To stand up for justice and peace, then, you must first find peace within yourself. You must then demonstrate peace to others, which means you can't make a stand for peace while you are warring with your neighbor, hating your coworker, or judging your boss."

Dr. Joe Dispenza

My observations:

Objective # 4:

I choose to resolve conflicts peacefully and give up the need to be right. I give space, cool down, and speak my truth without attacking.

(See pg. 152- Embrace Conflict as a Source of Growth and Transformation)

*I am developing the skill of letting go of outcome. I have learned how to truly listen. Rather than thinking of my response, I quiet my mind and just listen.
Sometimes it is better for me not to engage, to allow, and just observe what is*

"We repeat what we don't repair"
Tim Fletcher: YouTube Channel

I go to www.smoothtransitions4teens.com (ST4T) video channel: Interpersonal Skills/Personal Objectives and (Hope Journeys) video channel: Positive Relationship Approaches

Notes:

Objective # 5:

I decide to relate and work well with my employers, co-workers, teachers, schoolmates, family, friends, neighbors, strangers…

I go to: www.smoothtransitions4teens.com (ST4T) video channel: Interpersonal Skills/Personal Objectives and (Hope Journeys) video channel: Community Building Choices and Positive Relationship Approaches.

*If I have an issue with someone, I talk to them about it privately, in a respectful and direct manner. I maintain eye contact and no matter the response, I keep my cool. I deal with issues when they occur, if possible, rather than letting things go. Small problems can unnecessarily grow into bigger problems by waiting. Many times, it is only a matter of miscommunication or lack of communication. *

My successes:

REGULATING ACTIVITIES

That Reduce Stress and Anger:
The 6 R's

REPETITIVE (walking, puzzles, exercise, beading…)

RHYTHMIC (music, dance, rocking, yoga…)

RELEVANT (can see the benefit of doing it, working toward a goal, writing, reading, drawing…)

RELATIONAL (connects positively with something or someone)

RESPECTFUL (empowering and caring toward myself or others)

REWARDING (other short- and long-term benefits beyond helping me remain calm…)

SOURCE: NMT (Neurosequential Model of Therapeutics)-
Dr. Bruce Perry, Child Trauma Academy

I go to www.smoothtransitions4teens.com
(ST4T) video channel: Interpersonal Skills/Personal Objectives
and (Hope Journeys) video channel: Positive Relationship Approaches.

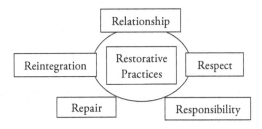

SOURCE: Teaching Peace by Beverly Title

"If we could read the secret history of our enemies, we should find in each man's life Sorrow and suffering enough to disarm all hostility."

Henry Wadsworth Longfellow
The Most Popular American Poet of His Day

Henry Wadsworth Longfellow was an American poet and educator. He lived from 1807-1882 in Portland, Maine. Longfellow began writing as a young child. He spent time in Europe, became a professor at Harvard, and spoke 7 different languages. He is generally regarded as the most distinguished poet America has ever produced. Many of his works helped shape the American character.

"Be not like dumb driven cattle, be a hero in the strife."

"The heights by great men reached and kept were not attained in sudden flight, but they, while their companions slept, were toiling upwards in the night."

"Man is unjust, but God is just, and finally, justice triumphs."

Source: YouTube- The Life Story of Henry Wadsworth Longfellow: The Story of Liberty

Those who deny freedom to others,
deserve it not for themselves:
and, under a just God,
cannot long retain it."

President Abraham Lincoln

Permission for use granted by city of Sterling, CO

LEGAL ISSUES

Warren Burger
Chief Justice of the United States Supreme Court 1969-1986

"Ever since people began living in tribes and villages,
they have had to balance order with liberty.
Individual freedom had to be weighed against
the need for security of all.

The delegates who wrote this Constitution in Philadelphia
in 1787 did not invent all the ideas and ideals it embraced,
but drew on the wisdom of the ages to combine the
best of the past in a conception of government of rule by
"We the People" with limits on government to
protect freedom.

This Constitution was not perfect; it is not perfect today even with amendments,
but it has continued longer than any other written form of government.
It sought to fulfill the promises of the Declaration of Independence of 1776,
which expressed peoples' yearning to be free and to develop the talents
given them by their Creator.

This Constitution creates three separate, independent branches of government,
with checks and balances that keep the power of government
within the boundaries set by law. This system does not always
provide tidy results; it depends on a clash of views in debate
and on bargain and compromise.

For 200 years this Constitution's ordered liberty has unleashed
the energies and talents of people
to create a good life."

SOURCE: Commission on the Bicentennial of the Unites States Constitution
The Constitution of the United States
and The Declaration of Independence
Warren Burger, Chairman
Chief Justice of the United States, 1969-1986

Objective # 1:

I create my alphabetically organized and lockable file box to store copies of important documents so I will have a backup. I keep it in a safe place.

I go to www.smoothtransitions4teens.com (ST4T) video channel: Employment/Legal Issues. I keep the original documents listed below that I do not need to carry with me locked up.

*I protect my identity. I keep my documents private and safe. I avoid giving personal financial information unless I initiate a transaction. I never use unsecured Wi-Fi to do any financial transaction. I never carry my social security card. I only give my social security number when I am sure it is safe and required *

DOCUMENT NAME	AGENCY CONTACT INFORMATION
Birth Certificate (Locked Box)	
Social Security Card (Locked Box)	
State Identity Card (if I need one), or Student ID (Carry with me)	
Driver's License (Carry with me)	
Work Permit if needed (Carry with me)	

Objective # 1 (continued):

I create my alphabetically organized and <u>lockable file box</u> to store <u>copies</u> of important documents, so I have a backup copy.

I keep it locked and in a safe place. I keep the <u>original documents</u> listed below that I do not need to carry with me <u>locked up.</u>

DOCUMENT NAME	AGENCY CONTACT INFORMATION

School Transcripts/ High School Diploma/ GED (Locked Box)

Other Degrees or Certificates (Locked Box)

Medical Records (Locked Box or File)

Registration for Selective Service, military service at age 18 (Males only) (Locked Box)
Failure to register is a felony punishable by a fine of up to $250,000, and/or 5 years in jail.

<u>I register to Vote at my local county courthouse.</u> *I bring my ID and proof of residence to register and obtain my Voter Registration Card. I know election dates and <u>my designated</u> local voting location. I study up on the candidates ahead of time. I am <u>an active participant in democracy.</u> I learn about <u>The Constitution</u>, "which has continued longer that any other written form of government." Chief Justice Warren Burger. <u>It is the supreme law of the land in the United States of America. I VOTE!</u>

Other Documents:

Objective # 2:

I check out potential career options for working in the criminal justice system such as attorney, judge, police officer, court reporter….

I go to <u>www.smoothtransitions4teens.com</u> (ST4T) video channel: Employment/Legal, (Hope Journeys) video channel: Criminal Justice and other resources.

FOUNDING FATHERS
of the United States of America

"Observe good faith and justice toward all nations. Cultivate peace and harmony with all."

"Truth will ultimately prevail where there is pains to bring it to light."

"If the freedom of speech is taken away, then dumb and silent we may be led, like sheep to the slaughter."

President George Washington

Revolutionary War General, Chair of the Constitutional Convention, first President of the United States

---

"I give you Independence Forever."

"The only maxim of a free government ought to be to trust no man living with power to endanger the public liberty."

"Liberty once lost, is lost forever."

"You will never know how much it cost the present generation to preserve your freedom! I hope you will make a good use of it"

*

On his death bed; July 4, 1826

"Thomas Jefferson survives"

Adams and Jefferson died on the same day July 4, 1826, the 50th anniversary of the Declaration of Independence

President John Adams

Leading Spokesperson for the adoption of the Declaration of Independence, ambassador to England, France, and Holland.

First Vice-President and second President of the United States.

Only 2 of the first 12 presidents never owned slaves, John Adams, and John Quincy Adams, sixth President of the United States: John Adams' son.

---

*"It rests now with ourselves alone to enjoy in peace and concord the blessings of self-government, so long denied to humankind: to show by example the sufficiency of human reason for the care of human affairs, and that **the will of the majority, the natural law of every society, is the only sure guardian of the rights of man.**"*

"His power of thought and expression brought us from our seats." Speaking of John Adams during the final debate which decided the vote for the Declaration of Independence. July 2nd, 1776

"I know of no danger so dreadful and so probable as that of internal contests, and I know no remedy so likely to prevent it as the strengthening of the band which connects us."

President Thomas Jefferson

Author of the Declaration of Independence, second Vice-President and third President of the United States. Founder of the University of Virginia, strong proponent along with President James Madison of freedom of religion

---

"To succeed, jump as quickly at opportunities as you do at conclusions. Do not anticipate trouble or worry about what may never happen. Keep in the sunlight."

At the conclusion of the Constitutional Convention Benjamin Franklin was asked, "What have you wrought?", he answered, "… a Republic, if you can keep it."

Benjamin Franklin

Author, Politician, Ambassador to France, Scientist, Inventor, Statesman

---

"The sacred rights of mankind are not to be rummaged for,
among old parchments, or musty records.
They are written, as with a sun beam in the whole volume
of human nature, by the hand of the divinity itself;
and can never be erased or obscured
by mortal power."

Alexander Hamilton

First Secretary of the Treasury, main proponent of a central bank, served as second in command under General George Washington in the Revolutionary War.

"Don't let the fear of striking out hold you back."

Babe Ruth Professional Baseball Player
George Herman Ruth, 'the Babe', One of The Best Athletes of All Time

George Herman Ruth was born in Baltimore, Maryland in 1895. Son of a bartender, this incorrigible young boy was routinely in trouble. He attended the St. Mary's school for boys, starting at age 7, where he joined the baseball team. George was a stand-out. By 1914, at age 19, he signed with the Baltimore Orioles, a minor league team at the time, but was soon 'sold' to the Boston Red Sox.

Unknown to many, Ruth was an excellent pitcher, winning 23 games in 1916, including 9 shut outs. His Red Sox won the World Series that year, in part due to the Babe's pitching.

Babe went on to win 24 more games in 1917, used only sparingly as a hitter. By 1918 his hitting career started to take off, helping the Red Sox claim 3 World Series championships.

The Red Sox traded Ruth to the New York Yankees following the 1919 season for a staggering $100,000, a sum unheard of at that time. Ruth and the Yankees went on to phenomenal success as the Babe broke his old record of 29 homers, slugging 54 in the 1920 season.

He was a superstar, fans flocked to the polo grounds. At one game more than 15,000 fans were turned away due to lack of seating. One million tickets sold that season, a first for any team. The new Yankee stadium was built to handle the crowds. It came to be known as the house that Ruth built.

The 1920's saw Babe Ruth become one of the most enduring sports figures of all time, loved by millions and idolized by the many children who flocked to him. Heck, he was a big kid himself, and the kids couldn't get enough of him.
During the 1927 season, Babe walloped 60 homers, a record which stood until 1960, when Roger Maris topped him, slugging 61. During his career the Yankees played in 7 World Series, winning 4.

Ruth was a free-spending, heavy drinking partier who was known for tipping generously and was very popular with women, for which he paid in his married life. The great bambino died of cancer in 1948 at the age of 53. An estimated 77,000 people filed past his casket at Yankee Stadium to pay their respects.

Ruth was Home Run King for many decades, until Maris, then hammerin' Hank Aaron, who spoke out against pervasive racism in major league baseball, broke the record. Aaron surpassed the Babe and Roger Maris' titles with 755 homers. Barry Bonds later exceeded the record with 762. Dozens of books have been written about Babe Ruth. Films have been made about his life. In short, millions of people the world over loved the great bambino.

Source: YouTube- Babe Ruth Biography: Reading Through History

'Riders on the Plains' Permission granted by Artist Steve Parrish and the City of Sterling, CO.

LEISURE AND RECREATION

Objective # 1:

I do any kind of exercise I enjoy several times a week.

I go to www.smoothtransitions4teens.com (ST4T) video channel: Leisure and Recreation, or I just start my exercise habit if I'm not already active.

"You become what you do every day."
Aristotle

Activities:

Objective # 2: Date(s):

I enter recreation activities I participate in on my phone and/ or calendar.

Objective # 3:

I find positive, new, creative recreation outlets for myself. I check online, researching available local possibilities that interest me.

*I may hike, bike, swim, kayak, jog, shoot hoops, walk dogs, or play with puppies at an animal shelter, coach, mentor kids, golf, play ping pong or tennis, weightlift, play soccer, baseball, dance...

* My activities:

Objective #4:

I may join a team or volunteer to help a sports or recreation group. *This could be a good way to meet people and make friends*

I go to www.smoothtransitions4teens.com (ST4T) video channel: Leisure and Recreation or Volunteering for ideas if I need to.

Information:

Objective #5:

I learn how to swim or become a better swimmer. It's a great way to relax.

I go to www.smoothtransitions4teens.com (ST4T) video channel: Leisure and Recreation if needed.

Notes:

Objective # 6:

I go camping and learn my survival skills.

I learn how to build a campfire, cook over a fire, and may help set up a tent. I check out videos on how to read a compass, a map, and take time to connect with nature and enjoy the outdoors

I go to www.smoothtransitions4teens.com (ST4T) video channel: Leisure and Recreation. Dates, locations, and skills learned:

Objective # 7:

I check out careers in coaching, athletic training, sports broadcasting, sports medicine, professional sports, sports podcasting/journalism, sports management…. If I am interested.

I go to www.smoothtransitions4teens.com (ST4T) video channel: Leisure and Recreation.

Objective # 8:

I take time to read or write, journal, draw or paint, rest, relax; I just enjoy silence.

*I use my time well. <u>I pace myself</u>.

I reserve a quiet time for myself each day <u>without electronics</u>. Sometimes I like to walk in a park in the sunshine, spend time near water, just being outside.

"Never give up!
Failure and rejection are only the
first step to succeeding."

Jim Valvano
Heroic college championship-winning basketball coach

Myra Vandy

Author, Trainer, Consultant, True Friend, and
Mom In-Deed, to Over 300 Young People

"When I first started playing basketball, I was happy to make one basket. I found that the more I practiced, the better I got, and the more I enjoyed it.

About a year after I started 'shooting hoops', I made 23 left and right-handed hook shots near the three-point line in about 45 minutes one day. That felt great!

I am learning that when I apply this same approach to other parts of my life, those areas improve too. The more I practice, the easier it becomes.

I didn't give up, and that has made all the difference!"

"Everything you have in your life,
you have attracted to yourself
because of the way you think,
because of the person that you are.
You can change your life because
you can change the way you think."
<u>Brian Tracy</u>

MONEY MANAGEMENT

"Gratitude for the present moment and the
fullness of life now is true prosperity.
It cannot come in the future.
Then, in time, that prosperity manifests for you in various ways.

Eckhart Tolle: 'The Power of Now'
New York Times best-selling author, world renowned speaker,
spiritual teacher

Objective # 1:

I write out my monthly budget. I subtract expenses from my income. *When things change, I write a new budget. <u>I subtract my expenses from my total income</u>*

I go to www.smoothtransitions4teens.com (ST4T) video channel: Money Management.

MONTHLY BUDGET

<u>EXPENSE</u>	<u>ENTRY</u>	AMOUNT <u>SPENT</u>
Savings		
Food		
Rent		
Electric		
Gas / Water / Sewer		
Cable/Satellite		
Phone/ Cell Phone		
Wi-Fi / Internet access		
Health/Dental Insurance		
Medical/Dental Bills		
Credit Card payment		
Car Insurance		
Car Payment		
Car Maintenance		
Gasoline		
Clothing		
Entertainment		
Other		

TOTAL OF ALL MY MONTHLY INCOME _____

—

EXPENSES _____

DOLLARS REMAINING _____

Objective # 1 (continued):

I write out my monthly budget. I subtract expenses from my income. *When things change, I write a new budget. I subtract my expenses from my total income*

MONTHLY BUDGET

EXPENSE	ENTRY	AMOUNT SPENT
Savings		
Food		
Rent		
Electric		
Gas / Water / Sewer		
Cable/Satellite		
Phone/ Cell Phone		
Wi-Fi / Internet access		
Health/Dental Insurance		
Medical/Dental Bills		
Credit Card payment		
Car Insurance		
Car Payment		
Car Maintenance		
Gasoline		
Clothing		
Entertainment		
Other		

TOTAL OF ALL MY MONTHLY INCOME _____

EXPENSES _____

DOLLARS REMAINING _____

Objective # 2:

I practice balancing an imaginary checkbook by creating monthly scenarios for myself. *
I include my paycheck and other deposits, interest, expenses, including rent, electric, phone, gas, other bills, etc. I talk to someone with experience and ask for help if I need it. Whether I do my banking online or use a traditional checkbook, I balance my account at least monthly. I use online videos to train myself as needed. *

I go to www.smoothtransitions4teens.com (ST4T) video channel: Money Management.

Check Number	Date	Description of Transaction	Payment or Withdrawal	Fee (+/-)	Deposit/Credit or Interest	Balance	

Objective # 2 (continued):

I practice balancing an imaginary checkbook by creating monthly scenarios for myself. *

Check Number	Date	Description of Transaction	Payment or Withdrawal	Fee (+/-)	Deposit/Credit or Interest	Balance	

Objective # 3:   Date: _____

I open a savings account and/or an interest checking account for myself.

I go to www.smoothtransitions4teens.com (ST4T) video channel: Money Management.

*I save a minimum of _____ % of my income each month if someone else is paying my bills. Otherwise, I do my best to save ___% each month.

I write out my savings plan. *

MY SAVINGS PLAN

My age now: _____

Number of months until I will be on my own.
(I use my phone calendar.)   _____

Total number of months worked.   _____

Dollars per month I will save =   _____

Additional money saved from extra hours worked,
i.e., additional summer work hours, overtime,
other sources:

TOTAL   _____

Objective # 4   Date(s):_____

I commit to paying my bills on time.

*<u>I keep a record of bills I have paid</u>. If I am ever billed twice for something I have already paid for, I will have a paper and/or electronic record to prove I have already paid the bill.

I check my paycheck deductions for accuracy regularly.

Objective # 5:

I learn about establishing credit.
I do online research and talk to people I trust about the necessity, benefits, risks, and wise use of credit
I go to <u>www.smoothtransitions4teens.com</u> (ST4T) video channel: Money Management and other resources.

Notes:

Objective # 6:

I establish credit by age 21. I will need credit to rent a hotel room, rent a car or buy anything which I pay for over time, such as furniture, a car, a house, etc.

I go to www.smoothtransitions4teens.com (ST4T) video channel: Money Management and other resources.

*I avoid paying interest on credit card balances. I pay off my bill every month to establish good credit and boost my credit rating. I charge only what I must and am able to pay off before the monthly bill comes due. Interest rates on credit card balances are very expensive.

My credit score is the number which is calculated by banks or other lending agencies to determine if I am a good credit risk based on my credit history. I need to establish a credit history*

Notes:

Objective # 7:

I research career options in financial management, banking, accounting, business, stocks trader, and careers that address economic justice and social inequality.
I go to www.smoothtransitions4teens.com (ST4T) video channel: Money Management and (Hope Journeys) video channel: Social Justice/Economic Justice and other resources.

*Ideas * Plans * Information * Notes*

*"The measure of who
we are is what we do
with what we have."*

Vince Lombardi
Legendary NFL Coach, Leader, and Executive

In 1959 Vince Lombardi was named NFL Coach of the Year during his rookie season as the Green Bay Packers head coach. In 1970, Lombardi was posthumously inducted into the pro football hall of fame. In 1971, the Super Bowl trophy was renamed the Vince Lombardi trophy.

As a boy Vince worked for his father at the family butcher shop in New York. He didn't like it, but moving hefty sides of beef helped him build muscle that would help him later in his athletic career.

The young Brooklynite's football skills caught the eye of Fordham University. Fordham granted him a scholarship, even though he was considered undersized at 5"8", and 180 pounds. Vince went on to be a star member of the team.

Lombardi was 45 years old when he became head coach of the Green Bay Packers. Under his leadership the Packers never lost a season and won the first two Super Bowls in 1966 and 1967. Vince won a total of 5 NFL championships.

Lombardi experienced discrimination as an Italian American and used his influence as an NFL championship coach to fight for equality for his players on and off the field. He believed that players should be judged solely by their performance on the field. He supported fair housing bills in Wisconsin and even traded players who refused to accept the Packers stand on equality.

Vince Lombardi is considered one of the greatest football coaches of all time. Vince is also considered one of the greatest coaches and leaders in the history of American sports.

Sources: YouTube-Interesting Facts about Super Bowl Coach Vince Lombardi:
Successful Daily Habits.com

MY PERSONAL OBJECTIVES

"This chance will stand before you only once."

**<u>"The family unit plays a critical role in our society and
in the training of the generation to come."</u>**

*"The framers of the Constitution were so clear in the federalist papers and elsewhere
that they felt an independent judiciary was critical to the success of the nation."*

*Sandra Day O'Conner-
First female Supreme Court Justice 1981-2006*

Sandra Day O'Connor was an American attorney, politician, and jurist who served as an associate justice of the Supreme Court of the United States from 1981 to 2006. She was America's first female Supreme Court justice, and the first female majority leader of any state legislative upper house.

O'Connor was born in El Paso, Texas in 1930. Her parents owned a cattle ranch in southeastern Arizona, the largest and most successful ranch in the region. In the beginning, the remote ranch did not have electricity or running water. Living in such a remote area, school options were limited. She had already shown that she was quite bright. By age four, Sandra learned how to read. Her parents sent her to El Paso, Texas to live with her grandmother to attend school. She graduated high school when she was sixteen.

After graduating high school in 1946, O'Conner applied to Stanford University. She excelled and became Senior Class President at Stanford. Sandra finished two degrees in just six years, instead of seven. She graduated in 1950 with a bachelor's degree in economics and received her law degree in 1952. While in law school, O'Conner was a member of the board of editors for the *Stanford Law Review*, a very high honor for a law student. Upon graduation, she was at the top of her class, graduating third out of 102 students, only two places behind a fellow law student and friend, who went on to become Supreme Court justice, William H. Rehnquist.

Sandra Day O'Conner (1930-2023)
SOURCE: https://oconnorinstitute.org/civic-programs/oconnor-history/sandra-day-oconnor-policy-archives-research-library/biography/

My Personal Goals

* I Think and Create*

I express myself and experience life with joy.
I am getting to know myself better.
As I think, so I am.
I go to www.smoothtransitions4teens.com (ST4T) video
channel: Interpersonal Skills / Personal Objectives

*I AM Being Myself *

"Empty your mind, be formless and shapeless, like water."

Bruce Lee
Martial Arts Icon

I AM...

"Go confidently in the direction of your dreams!
Live the life you've imagined."
Henry David Thoreau
Author

*Ideas * Plans * Information * Notes*

"This is a time in history when it is not
enough to simply know;
This is a time to know how."

Dr. Joe Dispenza

Highly Sought After, Successful Leader of Self - Healing Seminars Worldwide

Dr. Joe Dispenza is the son of Sicilian immigrants. His family arrived in the US during the 1930's, in New York. They settled in the New Jersey suburbs. His parents were very supportive of Joe and his brother. If a mistake was made when young Joe failed at something, his dad would say "No big deal, try again." Whatever their interests were, their parents would support them. Joe was blessed to have a very happy home. Growing up in this supportive atmosphere, the future Dr. Dispenza learned to think outside of the box, was not afraid to fail, and became a great parent himself.

As a young doctor, Joe suffered a life-changing accident on his bicycle during a bike race. His back was severely injured. Four doctors recommended radical back surgery. Joe rejected all four opinions and decided not to have surgery. His father, who was by his side, said to the doctor, "Don't worry, he knows exactly what he's doing".

Joe repeated over and over to himself ***"The Power that made the body heals the body."*** He said, ***"the life force is a conscious intelligence and orchestrates so many functions that happen on a subconscious level."*** He was now challenged to live the things he philosophically and intellectually understood. ***"I think it usually takes tragedy to get to that point where we can't go on with business as usual".***

Dispenza knew the power of the sub-conscious mind and believed in that intelligence that gives life to the body. He did not want to let any thought in that he did not want to create for his future. He focused 2 hours a day in the morning and 2 hours at night. In 10 ½ weeks, Dr. Joe was back on his feet. At 11 weeks he was back at his practice and at 12 weeks he was training again.

Dr. Joe Dispenza and his team provide life-changing training sessions all over the world with miraculous results. Inner powered self-healing from all sorts of diseases, trauma, and other afflictions have taken place. Dr. Joe and his team use the scientifically proven methods of epigenetics, psychoimmunology, quantum physics and more to assist training participants along their self-healing journey.

Source: YouTube- The Joe Dispenza Story.avi- 'My Childhood and How to Become a Great Parent'

*"The Universe is a big Dream Machine, turning out dreams
and transforming them into reality, and our own dreams are
inextricably woven into the overall scheme of things."*

Dr. Deepak Chopra

Widely Sought after Teacher and Trainer
of the Mind Body Connection

Bestselling author, native of India, son of a doctor, Deepak Chopra was sent to New York at age 14. He had eight dollars when he left India. His father wanted him to become a doctor, but Deepak wanted to become a writer. Deepak's father sent him to connect with associates at a New Jersey hospital. His uncle gave him one hundred dollars when he got as far as London, but he spent every bit of it at the Moulin Rouge cabaret in Paris. Upon arrival Deepak made a collect call to the hospital where they were awaiting his arrival. He was promptly picked up and ferried from the airport to the hospital by helicopter, totally dazzled by the bird's eye view of Manhattan.

Dr. Chopra began as an emergency room intern. After that he became an instructor of medicine at the Boston University Medical Center. In 1993 he founded The Chopra Center for Wellbeing in partnership with another doctor. Dr. Chopra is a widely sought after teacher/trainer of meditation, emotional wellbeing, understanding the mind-body connection and consciousness.

*"Every time you react the same old way,
ask if you want to be a prisoner of the past or
a pioneer of the future."*

Source: YouTube: Dr. Deepak Chopra, Life, Career and Universe? Fortune; Fortune Magazine

TRANSPORTATION

Objective #1:

I go online to check out public transportation if I need it.

Notes, Date(s):

Objective # 2   Date: _____

I get my driver's license by age 18 if I choose to. I do so while still in high school, if possible, to take advantage of free drivers ed training where available.

I go to www.smoothtransition4teens.com (ST4T) video channel: Transportation.

Objective # 3   Date: _____

I research car buying and check blue-book values online (average buying and selling prices for cars based on age, condition, etc.).
I go to www.smoothtransition4teens.com (ST4T) video channel: Transportation.

*I compare and shop around before buying anything. I take my time; talk to people I trust who are experienced in car buying.
I know the total cost of my car, including total interest costs, insurance, and maintenance.

Notes:

Objective # 4: Date: _____

I research vehicle insurance. I go online and get several rate quotes before I buy a vehicle. I shop around.
I go to www.smoothtransition4teens.com (ST4T) video channel: Transportation.

*I talk to people I trust, ask them where they buy insurance and what their experiences have been to get the best value I can. *

Notes:

Things that May Affect Insurance Rates
Level of Insurance Coverage
Deductible Amount
Age
Previous Car Insurance Claims
Demographics (including Marital Status)
Credit History
Driving History
Annual Mileage
Car Make and Model
ZIP Code

"Travel is the only thing you can buy that makes you richer."

Saltinourhair.com

Objective # 5: Date: _____

I get to know a good mechanic. I check online reviews, ask around, talk to friends, family, and acquaintances.

I go to www.smoothtransition4teens.com (ST4T) video channel: Transportation.

*I have my mechanic check out a vehicle before I buy it. I resist the temptation to buy the first thing I like. I take the time to shop around to compare prices, models, and costs of maintaining the vehicle I may be interested in buying.
* The main thing I must be sure of is, can I afford all costs associated with owning, insuring, and maintaining the vehicle.

Record information:

Objective # 6: Date(s): _____

I read the owner's manual for my vehicle. I keep it in my glove compartment and become familiar with my vehicle.

I go to www.smoothtransition4teens.com (ST4T) video channel: Transportation.

I make sure I keep my car serviced. Scheduled service times for oil changes, transmission, engine coolant etc. are listed in my owner's manual. I spend the money to keep my car serviced. My car will last a lot longer and I will avoid costly repairs. I will save money in the long run

Objective # 7

I explore career options in the transportation industry: trucking, shipping, automotive careers, air transport, space, new technology development...
I research these potential career options on my own and

I go to www.smoothtransitions4teens.com (ST4T) video channel:
Transportation and other resources.

*"All our dreams can come true If we have the
courage to pursue them."*

Walt Disney

Creative Genius of Cartoons, Animated Movies, Entrepreneur, Television Host, Creator of Disneyland, and Disneyworld

Walt Disney spent his childhood honing his art skills, coloring, drawing newspaper cartoons, water coloring, and taking art lessons. He was the cartoonist for his high school newspaper.

Walt worked hard to break into animation. He developed his own company, then went to Hollywood. He formed Disney Brothers Studios and created Mortimer Mouse, AKA Mickey Mouse…

At Disney Brothers Studios, Walt brought in animators to produce cartoons. In 1931, he suffered a nervous breakdown. By 1937 he bounced back with Snow White and the Seven Dwarfs, then Pinocchio, Fantasia, and Bambi. Walt was tough on his employees and was criticized for perpetuating black stereotypes. In the late 1950's and 1960's Walt hosted television shows; first Disneyland, later Walt Disney Presents, then The Wonderful World of Color.

Disney's crowning achievements were movies like Mary Poppins, but especially Disneyland and Disneyworld.

A heavy smoker, Walt Disney sadly passed, before the opening of Disneyworld and The Epcot Center.

*"The way to get
started is to
quit talking and get busy."*

Source: YouTube- The Fascinating True Story of Walt Disney; Ms Mojo

*"Youth can always make a significant contribution
to the development of the communities
in which they live.
What is needed for this to happen
are specific projects that will connect youth with the community."*

Professor John McKnight

Author, Visionary, and Practitioner of Simple Yet Ingenious
Methods for Sustainable, True Community Building -
"*Drawn from local citizens who identify their
community assets rather than deficits."
<u>"Next mobilize to work together on the things
they care enough about to act upon"</u>

Source: Building Communities from the Inside Out: A path Toward Finding and
Mobilizing a Community's Assets: John P. Kretzmann and John McKnight

VOLUNTEERING

Benefits of Volunteerism

Research done by Carnegie Mellon University shows that volunteerism **_helps improve mood_** and may cause a release of the endorphins that are **_powerful antidotes to stress, a key to happiness and optimism_** and **_a way to combat feelings of helplessness and depression, promoting emotional well-being_**.

A national survey that led to the definition of the 'healthy-helper syndrome' showed two phases- one: **_an "immediate physical feel-good sensation,"_** and the other: **_a sense of calmness and relaxation._**

The research concluded that volunteers who experienced **_the 'healthy-helper syndrome'_** noticed **_an improvement in physical ailments as well as elevation of mood and feelings of well-being._**

Other factors that influence the positive health effects of volunteering include:

1. The desire to volunteer, which **_can strengthen the volunteer's sense of control._** Studies show that **_even when a volunteer doesn't particularly want to engage in volunteer work, they still reap positive health benefits if they continue the altruistic behavior._**

2. **_Volunteering_** for something a person likes doing, which **_brings pleasure._**

3. **_Consistency- the greatest health benefits appear to be reaped by those who do consistent, regular volunteer work._**

SUGGESTIONS FOR MAKING VOLUNTEERISM POSITIVE AND ENJOYABLE

- Encourage independence- give volunteer decision-making control in what and how projects are to be accomplished, whenever possible
- Give clear responsibilities.
- Break down complicated tasks into small, easy steps.
- Allow mistakes and reward efforts, even if results fall short of expectations.
- Increase volunteer's independence as proficiency with task is demonstrated.
- Be available to help if needed.

Source:
'Altruism and Health', MIND/BODY HEALTH, The Effects of Attitudes, Emotions and Relationships by Brent, Q. Hafen, Keith J. Karren, Kathryn J. Frandsen and N. Lee Smith

Objective # 1:

I Research volunteer possibilities I might be interested in online, in person, or through other methods. I check out career options through volunteering before I commit to a career or education plan.

I go to www.smoothtransition4teens.com (ST4T) video channel: Internships/ Volunteering and (Hope Journeys) video channel for potential volunteer opportunities.

"I slept and dreamt that life was joy.
I awoke and saw that life was service.
I acted and behold,
Service was joy."
Tagore
Nobel Prize Winner; Regarded as the Guru of Indian Literature

Volunteer Possibilities

Volunteer Site Name:

Volunteer Site Address:

Volunteer Site Contact Information (website, email):

Volunteer Site Telephone Number:

Supervisor Name(s):

Volunteer Coordinator:

Position Title:

Description of Responsibilities:

Number of hours per week/month:
Wages/Stipend:

Objective # 1 (continued):

I Research volunteer possibilities. *I check out career options through volunteering before I commit to an education plan. The people I volunteer with may have had many previous career experiences which I can learn from. (See pg. 210 Professor John McKnight quote.)

*The more possibilities I check out, the more likely I am
to find the perfect opportunity for myself *

Volunteer Possibilities

Volunteer Site Name:

Volunteer Site Address:

Volunteer Site Contact Information (website, email):

Volunteer Site Telephone Number:

Supervisor Name(s):

Volunteer Coordinator:

Position Title:

Description of Responsibilities:

Number of hours per week/month:

Wages/Stipend:

Objective # 2:   Date(s): _____

I participate in volunteer placement field trips. *I try out several possibilities and see what feels comfortable for me*.

I go to www.smoothtransition4teens.com (ST4T) video channel: Internships/Volunteering

Volunteer Placement Field Trips

Volunteer Site Name:

Volunteer Site Address:

Volunteer Site Contact Information (website, email):

Volunteer Site Telephone Number:

Supervisor Name(s):

Volunteer Coordinator:

Position Title:

Description of Responsibilities:

Number of hours per week/month:

Wages/Stipend:

Objective # 2 (continued):   Date(s): _____

I participate in volunteer placement field trips. *I try out several possibilities and see what feels comfortable for me*.

A field trip allows me to quickly eliminate some choices and move forward with an option which feels better*

Volunteer Placement Field Trips

Volunteer Site Name:

Volunteer Site Address:

Volunteer Site Contact Information (website, email):

Volunteer Site Telephone Number:

Supervisor Name(s):

Volunteer Coordinator:

Position Title:

Description of Responsibilities:

Number of hours per week/month:

Wages/Stipend:

Objective # 3:

I go on volunteer placement <u>interviews</u>.

<u>*I take SMOOTH TRANSITIONS 4 TEENS with me</u>. <u>I tell what I have accomplished and show the plans I have been working on.</u>

I am prepared to explain why I would like to volunteer.
I present myself with confidence and a smile.

Notes:

Objective # 4:   Date(s): _____

I carry out my volunteer work, possibly with a mentor, 3 or more hours per month.

*I try a variety of volunteer opportunities.
I meet great people and have opportunities to experiment with potential education and career options. I include my volunteer work in my resume`*

I go to www.smoothtransitions4teens.com (ST4T) video channel: Internships / Volunteering

"Never doubt that a small group of thoughtful,
committed, citizens can change the world.
Indeed, it is the only thing that ever has."

Margaret Mead

Volunteer Work

Volunteer Site Name:

Volunteer Site Address:

Volunteer Site Telephone Number:

Volunteer Site Contact Information (website, email):

Supervisor Name(s):

Volunteer Coordinator:

Position Title:

Description of Responsibilities:

Number of hours per week/month:

Wages/Stipend:

Objective # 4:   Date(s): _____

<u>I carry out</u> my volunteer work, possibly with a mentor, 3 or more hours per month.

I try a variety of volunteer opportunities. <u>Volunteering looks great on my resume' and could connect me with paid job opportunities</u>

"There is a debt of service due from every man to his country, proportioned to the bounties which nature and fortune have measured to him."

President Thomas Jefferson

Volunteer Work

Volunteer Site Name:

Volunteer Site Address:

Volunteer Site Telephone Number:

Volunteer Site Contact Information (website, email):

Supervisor Name(s):

Volunteer Coordinator:

Position Title:

Description of Responsibilities:

Number of hours per week/month:

Wages/Stipend:

Objective # 5:

I practice volunteer maintenance skills: appearance, accuracy, punctuality, working as a team member. *The qualities of character I display will speak volumes about the kind of person I am. People will take notice of the employment skills I regularly demonstrate *

I go to www.smoothtransition4teens.com (ST4T) video channel: Internships/Volunteering, and other sources.

Notes:

Objective # 6:

I ask for letters of reference for future employment or academic references before I leave a volunteer site.

* I thank those I have volunteered with for the opportunity to work alongside them. If I think it is appropriate, certain fellow volunteers might be a good source for letters of reference*

"You can easily judge the character of a man by how he treats those who can do nothing for him."

Johann Wolfgang von Goethe

Information and date(s):

"No one can make you feel inferior without your consent." ...

"Surely, in the light of history, it is more intelligent to hope rather than to fear, to try rather than not to try. For one thing we know beyond all doubt: Nothing has been achieved by the person who says, 'It can't be done'."

Eleanor Roosevelt

First Lady of the United States 1933-1945.
Unique American Leader, Activist, Special Envoy
to President Franklin Delano Roosevelt

Anna Eleanor Roosevelt was born on October 11, 1884. Her mother died from <u>diphtheria</u> in 1892. Her father, an alcoholic confined to a sanitarium, died in 1894, after jumping from a window during a fit of <u>delirium tremens</u>. He survived the fall but died from a seizure.

Eleanor's childhood losses left her prone to depression throughout her life. Her brother Hall later suffered from alcoholism. ***<u>A shy, awkward child, starved for recognition and love, Eleanor Roosevelt grew into a woman with great sensitivity to the underprivileged of all creeds, races, and nations.</u>*** Her constant work to improve their lot made her one of the most loved—and for some years ***<u>one of the most revered—women of her generation.</u>***

Though widely respected in her later years, Roosevelt was ***<u>a controversial first lady at the time for her outspokenness, particularly on her promotion of civil rights for African-Americans.</u>***

She was the first presidential spouse to hold regular press conferences, write a daily newspaper column, write a monthly magazine column, host a weekly radio show, and speak at a national party convention.

<u>"Courage is more exhilarating than fear and in the long run easier.</u> *We do not have to become heroes overnight. Just one step at a time, meeting each thing that comes up, seeing it not as dreadful as it appeared, discovering **<u>we have the strength</u>** to stare it down"*.

SOURCE: <u>https://www.fdrlibrary.org/er-biography</u>

*Ideas * Plans * Information * Notes*

Authors' Challenge

Young people all around the world are coming of age in this era of the existential perils of climate crisis, social, and political upheaval. They are inheriting huge challenges.

These videos could spark an interest in potential career choices. Even if different career paths are chosen, many more people of all ages and stages of life are critically needed ***to contribute in some way to create healthier, more durable communities, especially for youth.***

A healthy community is where everyone acts to take care of each other.
Some can play an active part in a ***Circle of Support*** for a young person by ***volunteering, mentoring,*** or by ***providing a job shadowing, internship, or employment opportunity. Others may contribute financially, invest in worthy initiatives, start a support group, host a potluck, have a block party...***

We stand at the crossroads of participation and observation. To be active citizens in a healthy democracy or passive consumers.

Conditions can never improve for anyone until he or she demands the *proper outcome*. Success in these efforts is certain as citizens act - casting out all doubt and fear.

Hope Journeys Social Improvement Career Options Videos

Climate Crisis / Environmental Justice

Criminal Justice: Police Reform / Prison Reform

Earth Stewardship: Air / Food / Soil / Water

Restoration / Reconstruction

Social Justice / Economic Justice

Hope Journeys Community Building Choices Videos

Asset Based Community Development – ABCD

Circle Process

Hope Journeys Positive Relationship Approaches Videos

Restorative Practices / Restorative Justice

Neurosequential Model of Therapeutics- NMT

Crisis Intervention

I go to www.smoothtransitions4teens.com to access the (Hope Journeys) video channel.

MY PLANS

"The world of the future is in our making.
Tomorrow is now."

Eleanor Roosevelt
Activist, Political Leader, Courageous First Lady,
Groundbreaking Pioneer for Women

MY PLANS

Month:

Year:

MY PLANS

Month: Year:

MY PLANS

MY PLANS

Month: Year:

MY PLANS

5   Month: Year:

MY PLANS

MY PLANS

Month: Year:

MY PLANS

MY PLANS

Month:

Year:

MY PLANS

MY PLANS

Month: Year:

MY PLANS

MY PLANS

Month: Year:

MY PLANS

Month: Year:

MY PLANS

Month: Year:

MY PLANS

MY PLANS

Month: Year:

MY PLANS

Month: Year:

MY PLANS

Month: Year:

MY PLANS

20   Month: Year:

MY PLANS

Month: Year:

MY PLANS

MY PLANS

MY PLANS

Month: Year:

My Updated Survey

Date:

1. When I originally took the I Am Starting Survey I listed my hobbies and interests and how I spend my free time. What have I changed?
    What am I doing when I'm doing something I enjoy so much, I just lose track of time?

2. In the first survey I identified problems in my town and the world, and what I could do about them. I also wrote down good things I could give my support to.
    To answer those questions now I would say....

3. Today if I ask myself if I work better alone, with someone else, in a small group or in a large group and what I'm naturally good at I would respond...

4. Now that some time has passed, do I want to work for myself, a small company, or a corporation, or...; and where do I want to live?

5. My ideas today for my job or profession are:

My Updated Survey

6. What are my biggest challenges?

   Who helps me with them?

   What am I doing about them right now?

7. What is most important to me now?

   What is most important to me in preparing for my future?

8. Who encourages my dreams, or who challenges me when I mess up?

   Who loves me?

9. What is one thing I can do today to reach my goals to create my perfect life?

10. In five years, I...